Smart Talk

Smart Talk

THE ART OF SAVVY BUSINESS CONVERSATION

Roberta Roesch

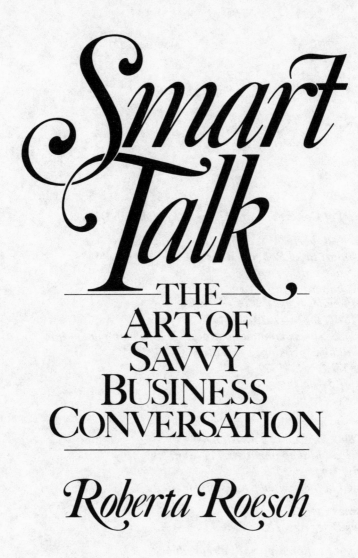

amacom
American Management Association

A James Peter Book
James Peter Associates, Inc.

Library of Congress Cataloging-in-Publication Data

Roesch, Roberta.
    Smart talk / Roberta Roesch.
        p.   cm.
    Bibliography: p.
    Includes index.
    ISBN 0-8144-7713-5
    1. Business communication.   2. Oral communication.
    3. Public speaking.   I. Title.
    HF5718.R64   1989
    651.7'3—dc20   89-45455
                                                                        CIP

A James Peter Book
James Peter Associates, Inc.

Preface

This book is the work of many people on the front lines of management. As a journalist and catalyst, I have but put together their views on how to develop the verbal communication skills that help advance a manager's career.

In researching the chapters that follow I interviewed a wide range of business people—managers and supervisors, CEOs and corporation presidents, and management consultants—as well as speech consultants; training directors; educators; communications experts; public relations counselors; and social and industrial psychologists. The book is a compilation of their advice.* Their plain-speaking, nuts-and-bolts tips are for managers just beginning a career as well as for those who are further along on their way to upper management.

Through real-life stories and typical corporate dialogues, you'll learn what to say, how to say it, and when and where to speak. You'll find out how to increase your visibility and display your upper-management potential. Moreover, these straightforward suggestions will work in every situation where your communication skills are vital to your effectiveness.

As I talked to people in business, I was struck by how often the successful strategies are also so simple—basically, such pure common sense. And always the bottom line is the same: Good verbal communication is based on good human relationships.

Many people shared in this book, but I owe special thanks to Marc Dorio, Mark Clemente, Dr. Paula Kurman, Laura Hart, Michael Levine, J. Porter Henry, Jr., Milo Sobel, Dr. Donald

---

*In most cases their real names have been used. But in a few instances anonymity was requested, and those requests have been honored.

Kirkpatrick, Don Christman, Marcy Syms, Phyllis Macklin, Dr. David Eyler, Doe Lang, Susan Hayes, Tony Cipollone, Don Bagin and Ed Moore of *communication briefings,* Toastmasters International, and International Training In Communication. I also thank my editors, Eva Weiss and Barbara Horowitz, for their counsel, encouragement, and editorial suggestions, and I thank my family—Phil, Jeff, Bonnie, and Meredith—for their continual help and support in all of my writing endeavors.

Contents

Contents

Contents

PART I

Your Verbal Strength

CHAPTER 1

What's Your Verbal IQ?

"The problem was . . . and here's how we solved it."

When the manager of a team of five in a medium-size insurance company learned that three of his staff were leaving, his instant comment to the remaining staff was, "With those *good* people out of here, where does that leave us?"

The two claims adjusters still on the team were offended by those words. And when the top manager learned of the remark, he said of the manager, "Let's hope he never goes into diplomacy, or he'll start a nuclear war."

In another situation, a systems analyst and department manager killed her advancement chances because she spent too much supervisory time talking about irrelevant things or rambling on and on. "She's never able to get to the point," her manager said of her, "so even though she's brilliant, she's perceived as a talker and not a doer."

In a third instance, a middle manager in a manufacturing company was caught off guard when he was criticized for mishandling a project. "You really messed up," his boss said. "What on earth happened here?"

3

The middle manager was angered by his boss's criticism and immediately responded defensively with, "The people I trusted to work with me must have misunderstood what we wanted. *They* were responsible for most of the job, so if you don't like the project, don't take it out on me."

"He couldn't take heat and keep his cool," the boss later said, "and his response certainly didn't show that, regardless of who was at fault, he'd try to solve the problem."

These people are victims of their own low verbal IQs, and the poor verbal skills and images they project to their senior executives and subordinates, as well as to their co-workers and peers, constantly work against them when they try to demonstrate their ability to think, evaluate, and explain.

By every business standard, well-handled verbal responses strengthen your visibility and showcase your upper-management potential. As a result, your verbal reactions to corporate challenges require as much skill and foresight as crafting a report to top management or writing a commendable memo.

In many years of researching and writing in the field of personal development, I've seen this to be true again and again, not only through observation but also as brought up in hundreds of interviews with top business leaders. This book is seasoned with real-life situations and advice from executives and managers. The chapters that follow cover specific situations that managers commonly face, specific ways they can speak up and handle those situations, and tested strategies and dialogues. In the early chapters you'll also find some short quizzes to get you started on speaking well with good verbal responses. Occasionally, there will be a quiz in later chapters as well.

What Constitutes a High Verbal IQ?

A high verbal IQ is the packaged result of your ability to speak effectively, with verbal fluency and flexibility. It's based on your being in control of your words—and the way you deliver them—as you face common situations in the business world.

"It's also built on brevity, accuracy, truthfulness—and humor in moderate doses," states Mark Clemente, a marketing director for an accounting and management consulting firm. "And since you keep your response businesslike and minimize personal discussions, it shows you're organized and on top of your job."

VERBAL IQ QUIZ

To determine the level of your verbal IQ, take the following quiz. Check the responses that apply to you, and score yourself at the end.

	A Always	B Sometimes	C Never
1. Do you know the right phrases to use when you encounter the un-expected?	____	____	____
2. Are you able to encourage shy or reserved people to open up and talk to you?	____	____	____
3. Do you know when to listen, when to talk, when to interrupt, and when to wait for a better time?	____	____	____
4. Can you keep your cool and deal with difficult situations calmly, constructively, and with an open mind?	____	____	____

5

	A Always	B Sometimes	C Never
5. Are you good at slipping key points about your accomplishments into your dialogue (especially if you feel you're being ignored)?	____	____	____
6. Do you refrain from using a disparaging manner in dealing with business colleagues?	____	____	____
7. Do you avoid pointless, routine statements?	____	____	____
8. Do you know how to get the rewards and credit you deserve for even your smallest achievements?	____	____	____
9. Do you focus on solutions rather than on problems and mistakes?	____	____	____
10. Do you come across to your co-workers as honest and sincere?	____	____	____
TOTALS	____	____	____

Scoring: Add up your A, B, and C answers. If the majority are A's, your verbal IQ is on the rise. But if your score is mostly

B's and C's (or overwhelmingly C's), you need to sharpen your verbal communication skills.

To further assess your Smart Talk skills, answer the following questions. Take plenty of time to develop your answers so that your subsequent evaluations can be honest and thorough. One technique that helps is to write one question on each of five large index cards. Then you can write your answers on each card, adding responses as you complete ongoing evaluations.

1. What is the overall effect you think you have on others when you speak to them?
2. In what situations do you find it most difficult to speak to senior executives, subordinates, or co-workers?
3. On what occasions have you communicated particularly well verbally, and why do you think things went so well those times?
4. When have you "goofed," and what were the underlying reasons for it?
5. What do you do when other people ignore or dismiss what you have said?

Why Your Verbal IQ Is Important

By every standard, a good verbal IQ enhances your image and sense of well-being. It gives you an opportunity to create or reinforce the valuable personal impact you have on people. It's a front-row ticket to management success. Since it helps you succeed with people, it determines to a great extent how satisfying, successful, and productive your working life will be.

Moreover, a good verbal IQ is important because the American work force is changing dramatically. In the past, management methods were often based on the assumption that workers were primarily white and male. But by the 1990s, 75 percent of those entering the work force will be women and minorities. Since these people will now constitute our corporations, government agencies, educational institutions, and other organizations, the key to management success lies in knowing how to communicate with—and manage and motivate—diverse employees in multicultural environments. Communicating across cultures is more important than ever if misunderstandings and conflicts are to be avoided. As David Kearns, CEO and president of Xerox Corporation, puts it: "The company that gets out in front managing diversity, in my opinion, will have a competitive edge."[1]

Beyond this, your verbal IQ illustrates your business judgment. As everyone knows, a manager moves up in the world because he or she has maturity and knowledge of subject matter. "Your potential as a senior manager is also determined by your judgment," declares Mark Clemente. "Every decision you make shows your thought processes, your sophistication in dealing with and responding to challenges, how you take situational variables into account, and the strategies and solutions you employ to overcome problems."

Project a Positive Verbal IQ

Each of the four elements for projecting a positive verbal IQ is covered in subsequent chapters, but let's consider them here briefly, because each is a four-star necessity for dealing with and responding to the collective demands of your business life.

1. *Prepare for every encounter.* "Your attitude has to be that every encounter is an important one and that your first three minutes can make or break you," advises Marc Dorio, vice-president of an international management consulting firm.

With this in mind, anticipate what is most likely to happen in your encounters with people and prepare possible scenarios.

8

Since nothing can be taken for granted, formulate specific *adaptable* verbal responses to subjects and questions that may come up. Write down what you want to cover. Then practice out loud what you plan to say and how you wish to say it. Think of all possible reactions to your words, and practice your replies to those reactions, making sure your responses sound appropriate and natural rather than rehearsed.

2. *Avoid talking too much.* "Sometimes you can divulge information you'd never have to give, simply because you're so open about it," says Dorio. "You give things you haven't been asked for. You say things that are wrong."

This happens in corporate settings every day, but it's most evident in courtrooms. For example, in the 1988 Bess Myerson trial, the former Miss America and New York City Cultural Affairs Commissioner, her friend Carl A. Capasso, and Justice Hortense Gabel were tried (and later acquitted) on charges that Myerson had hired Justice Gabel's daughter in exchange for a reduction in alimony payments resulting from Capasso's divorce case. When witnesses tried to talk too much and give answers to questions they hadn't been asked, the presiding judge pointed his finger at them and exclaimed impatiently, "I admonished you not to volunteer, just to answer the questions that are asked."

This is true in business, too.

3. *Keep the hierarchy straight.* When you're on the giving end of criticism and one of your subordinates makes an error, establish your authority immediately and let the subordinate know the mistake was his responsibility, and that you will not tolerate continuing mistakes. But create an environment that's conducive to solving the problem by giving subordinates the opportunity to come back with solutions. "Then, if they come back and the solution is still not right, well, they've had their chance," says Clemente.

"On the other hand, when subordinates fail to solve the problem, you have to step in with 'Here's the way I think it should be done.' Often I have the answers, but I don't tell my people that. I wait for them to come back with solutions. Then, even if their solution is not the correct way to go, it still shows me how sensitive to their responsibility they are and how persuasively they communicate ideas."

4. *Concentrate on solutions rather than on problems.* When you're on the receiving end of corporate criticism, show that you are working on a solution. Suppose, for instance, your manager says, "But this is horrible" when you've just given him your best work. "This reaction is never easy to take," continues Clemente. "You need to understand that people have different perceptions of quality." After presenting your best work, listen to feedback and take criticism constructively. Often, there's no real right or wrong. A good response can be "How can we make it better?" A bad response is to react defensively.

Naturally, it's legitimate to ask where you went wrong. It's equally legitimate to defend your action or decision if you had good reasons. In the latter case, explain your action. "An appropriate response is, 'Here's what I did; here's why I did it; here's what my thinking was,' " advises Clemente.

Once you've addressed the problem, though, don't dwell on it. Instead, focus on a solution as you try to get input from your boss. Many times the people to whom you report aren't sure what they're looking for. When you receive feedback, request a chance to come back with a solution or an improvement that will give your supervisor what she desires.

Your Verbal IQ Increases Your Visibility

As Dizzy Dean put it, "It ain't bragging if you've done it." There's nothing wrong with slipping a plug for your accomplishments into your dialogue. But the trick is to do it in a way that doesn't label you a braggart.

"The message you're looking to communicate is 'Look how good I am,' " says Mark Clemente. "But it has to be communicated implicitly. For example, suppose I want to write a management report about a successful press conference we held that attracted thirty reporters and got terrific coverage. I don't say explicitly 'Look at the great job I've done.' Instead, I say 'Here is the job that was assigned and here are the results.'

"The message should never be presented with 'We were great, we did this, we did that,' " he adds. "You talk about the goals, the strategy, and the results. Assuming the results are good, you illustrate your success through facts."

A few select adjectives or descriptive phrases are permissible, and Clemente suggests such approaches as:

"The problem was . . . and here's how we solved it."

"Owing to our thorough efforts, . . ."

"I hope you agree that this was a comprehensive effort that netted excellent results."

Another way to make yourself visible is to praise others when justified. This positions you as a fair person, and when your praise is honest and sincere—and based on work you genuinely admire—people appreciate your truthful words.

According to Dorio, another way to achieve visibility is to help your boss be successful. "Think ahead to anticipate his needs. Ask him what he'd like you to do and what has to be done. And speak well of your boss when you have a chance," Dorio suggests. When you can do this honestly—and without seeming to pat yourself on the back—you'll gain visibility fast.

CHAPTER 2

Listen to Your Voice

"I can hear you, Charlie—You don't need to shout."

The way you sound to others can strengthen your visibility, showcase your upper-management potential, and have tremendous impact on your business success.

On the positive side, a high-quality voice can show you are in control. It can:

- Attract attention to you and your needs
- Calm testy co-workers and angry colleagues
- Inform and persuade others by encouraging them to support your ideas
- Make the orders you give more palatable so they'll be carried out

On the negative side, a poor-quality voice can indicate you're out of control as you deal with your colleagues and supervisors. It can reflect the stress or adversity that sometimes arises from confrontations.

For instance, increased volume can show that you're angry and excited. A pitch that's too high can be evidence of nervousness and tension. Mumbling indicates that you're insecure and don't know how to respond, while slips of the tongue can cause others to think you may be confused and anxious.

Professor Harold Zullow, a psychologist at the University of Pennsylvania, is an expert on anxiety. During presidential campaigns he analyzes the speeches and verbal performances of the candidates. Zullow concluded that after the first 1988 Bush-Dukakis debate, Michael S. Dukakis was "markedly . . . anxious, a mood that affected his performance as well as the public's perception of him."[1]

The psychologist based his assessment of anxiety partly "on slips of the tongue, stuttering, repeating words, and frequent use of 'uh' and 'ah.' " He recalls his favorite campaign slip of the tongue, said during the 1980 presidential campaign. After losing his debate to Ronald Reagan in Cleveland, Jimmy Carter "thanked the city for its hospitality during the last hours of his life."[2]

According to Zullow, throughout the 1988 debates George Bush also displayed speech disturbances at a consistent rate, which suggests a politician "anxious in the public forum." The professor noted that in the first debate Bush made errors in 20 percent of his sentences; in the second debate, in 17 or 18 percent of his remarks.

In Zullow's view, Dukakis was "far more anxious in the second debate than he was in the first." In the second debate, his speech-disturbance rate went from 5½ percent to 11 percent, indicating that Dukakis "was capable of putting on a virtually flawless verbal performance" and had "tremendous self-discipline and verbal control," which, however, could break down as a result of emotional circumstances and defeat.[3]

HOW DO YOU SOUND?

Take this quiz to test your self-awareness of how you think you sound. Later in the chapter there will be ways to find out how you *really* sound. For now, check the responses that you think apply, and score yourself at the end.

	A Always	B Sometimes	C Never
1. Is your voice clear, steady, and confident?	___	___	___
2. Does your voice project vitality, enthusiasm, and energy?	___	___	___
3. Do you keep your pitch at a healthy "medium" level?	___	___	___
4. Do you sound direct and straightforward, as though you mean what you say?	___	___	___
5. Do you generally refrain from speaking in a flat monotone?	___	___	___
6. Do you avoid sounding patronizing and condescending?	___	___	___
7. Do you put people at ease through your verbal mannerisms?	___	___	___
8. Do you tone down the volume of your voice when you're tempted to speak too loudly?	___	___	___
9. Do you eliminate "uhs" and "ahs" when suggesting ideas or courses of action?	___	___	___

	A Always	B Sometimes	C Never
10. Do you pay sufficient attention to pronouncing words and names correctly?	____	____	____
TOTALS	____	____	____

Scoring: Add up your A, B, and C answers. If the majority are A's, your voice quality is relatively good. But if your score is mostly B's and C's (or overwhelmingly C's), you need to improve the quality of your voice.

Seven Tools for Improving the Way You Sound

Regardless of your score, there's always room for improvement. Wherever you are in management, make use of the following tools and techniques to upgrade your potential.

1. *Pay attention to your tone of voice.* Your voice intonation can reflect your state of mind and make you appear patronizing, conciliatory, humorous, sarcastic, vibrant, lifeless, persuasive, belligerent, defensive, condescending, or devious. Similarly, the tone of your voice can reflect indecision, inferiority, antagonism, authority, honesty, confidence, straightforwardness, and support and respect for another person's actions.

The tone you use should be a good match for the situation and topic you face. In his book *Speak Your Way to Success,* Arthur W. Sager, an executive speech consultant, suggests asking the following four questions as you choose your tone for a verbal approach:

1. Are you essentially conveying information?
2. Are you persuading someone to adopt a point of view?
3. Are you advocating a course of action?
4. Are you attacking a decision or a plan?[4]

"Whatever attitude your topic demands should be established and your tone must be appropriate to the topic and to your attitude toward it," Sanger stresses.

In speaking of the importance of tone, Dr. Paula Kurman, a consultant to industry and director of Communicational Judo, Inc., tells of a colleague who was elected to a school board and who, because of her attention to tone and the way she matched it to the situation, won the immediate admiration of the members of the board.

The woman was devoted to education and to giving children the best. When she walked into a hot political situation, she felt she had to raise some questions that challenged the superintendent of schools. He promptly asked her in a condescending tone, "Are you questioning my judgment?" The woman responded in a level, straightforward tone, "Yes, sir, I am. That's my job."

"The tone of her response was a small verbal bow to the superintendent's position," explains Kurman. "And because it was respectful, straight, and honest, it put the answer in a frame the superintendent could not contest."

2. *Watch your articulation.* Articulation is the way you shape sounds into words and the way you enunciate, accent, and pronounce those words. Good articulation will get you where you want to go. It's a plus for developing your verbal IQ, because only through pronouncing each vowel, consonant, and syllable can you express yourself readily and clearly and only then can you put yourself across with poise and confidence.

On the other hand, poor articulation produces a negative image and signals a minus for selling your management skills. As Sandy Linver, a speech specialist and consultant, says in her book, *Speak Easy—How to Talk Your Way to the Top,* "Slurred, sloppy articulation often reflects jumbled thoughts, vague ideas or indifference toward a subject. . . . Few highly motivated people who really want to sell their message have poor articulation."[5]

Unfortunately, many managers make errors in articulation and fall prey to bad voice habits. For example, Carl is a manager who found himself in a difficult spot. His long-time boss, Joe Smith, was suddenly replaced by someone named Wolfgang Wohlgelernter. From the start, Carl had problems pronouncing the name.

It wouldn't have been difficult for Carl to separate the name into syllables—*Wohl-ge-lern-ter*—and then to practice enunciating it according to its sounds. But the first time Carl saw the name he decided he could never pronounce it, so he didn't even try. He told his new boss that he couldn't pronounce the name. Then it became Carl's routine to say to the boss, "You'll have to pronounce it for me." And though the boss generally complied, he passed the word around that "if Carl can't make the effort to learn how to say a name, it doesn't tell me good things about his motivation to move to top management."

In another situation, Elaine had the habit of slurring her *ing*'s, as in "I'm goin' to do it," "You'll be gettin' it soon," and "I'm puttin' it together today." "She might as well scrape her fingernail across my office blackboard," Elaine's supervisor remarked. "Such a sloppy way of using her voice drives me up a wall. To me, Elaine is indifferent to communicating at her best."

3. *Control your pitch.* We all have a wide natural range of pitch, with upper and lower limits. But a well-handled pitch somewhere in the middle of that range shows control.

An elevated pitch spells tension and excitement; if you doubt this, just listen to sportscasters at the height of a baseball game.

At the other end of the spectrum, a pitch that is too low can make you sound apathetic and lethargic or else indicate such overconfidence that people think you don't need support for your actions. In between the upper and lower limits are such varieties as the gruff, strident pitch some men employ and the little-girl sound certain women maintain.

Susan, a junior account executive in an advertising firm, was tops in studying her clients' sales problems and in developing resolutions. But the sound of her voice turned some people off; her high, soft pitch made her sound like a little girl. "I'd like to promote Susan," her supervisor said, "but with her high-pitched, childish voice she's not taken seriously. I need someone in a senior post who sounds assertive."

Certainly for the sake of variety there will be times when you will want to change your pitch. You'll want to elevate your pitch to stimulate the people with whom you're talking; other times you'll want to lower it to achieve a certain effect. But most of the time you should strike a balance between your upper and lower limits. Try out a variety of pitches. When you find one that is pleasing and natural while at the same time pleasantly assertive and authoritative, concentrate on using that pitch.

4. *Monitor your volume.* Nervousness can produce a stressed, loud voice. This is the case with Charlie, a manager in investment research in a large financial institution. For reasons unknown to his colleagues, Charlie is hyperactive and agitated for much of the working day, and this shows in the way he shouts in order to be heard. When Charlie phones people in other offices, those at desks across the room can overhear Charlie's every word.

But there's a difference between shouting and projecting. Don't think that because your volume is loud you're getting through to your colleagues. Usually the opposite is true; too often, a loud voice bothers others to the point that they will turn you off. In Charlie's office, the constant refrain that he fails to hear is, "We're in the same room, Charlie!"

As with pitch, all of us have a wide volume range. Try out your range of volume and listen to the sound. That way you'll never speak as loud as Charlie or, at the other end of the spectrum, so soft your associates can't hear what you say.

5. *Project energy and enthusiasm.* A voice that sounds vibrant and animated shows vigor and vitality. This has tremen-

dous influence for informing and persuading others. In *Speak Easy—How to Talk Your Way to the Top,* Sandy Linver writes:

> I once listened to three executives from the head office of a giant corporation rehearsing presentations about their company which they were going to deliver to some computer experts. None of the executives was an expert in computers, but they were all powerful, influential men with no conceivable reason to apologize to anyone for their lack of expertise in one particular area. Yet each stood up and read his speech exerting no energy, no authority, and no awareness. When they had finished I said, "How do you expect a group of the nation's leading computer experts to believe that the top-level executives from this powerful corporation are so self-effacing they can barely be heard?"[6]

6. *Listen to your rhythm. Webster's Ninth New Collegiate Dictionary* defines *rhythm* as "an ordered recurrent alteration of strong and weak elements in the flow of sound and silence in speech." Most of us don't think of this in our day-to-day business encounters, but it's important to vary your rhythm of speech to avoid monotony. As Arthur W. Sager wrote in *Speak Your Way to Success,*

> The importance of rhythm in speech may be illustrated by the fact that each language has its peculiar and characteristic stress and tempo. French differs from German in this respect—Italian from Swedish. People are apt to think that rhythm distinguishes poetry from prose, but the contrast is actually between a regular and an irregular stress. Poetry has a regular, measurable pattern of stress; prose also has patterns, but they are irregular. However, when they are under emotional pressure, people tend to speak with an increasingly regular beat even in prose. English is capable of a great variety of rhythms; so you should take advantage of that potential as you speak.[7]

7. *Check your pace.* Pace is a vital element in verbal communication, since talking rapidly or slowly sends management different messages. A pace that's too rapid can spell anxiety, as does a high pitch. Also, if you speak so fast that you

gallop verbally, colleagues may not be able to decipher your words.

On the other hand, a pace that is too slow can signal that you're slow on the uptake and overly cautious. For instance, in a large pharmaceutical company, a team head was called to her manager's office to discuss what was to be "a very brief overview of the team's project." But the team head spoke so slowly as she measured out each word that the boss was soon chomping at the bit to have her finish. "Right or wrong," the boss declared, "I just can't stand a slow talker. To me it literally means the same as being a slow thinker."

Strive for that middle ground—not too fast and not too slow—and vary your pace as you speak. When you feel you're not communicating, pick up the pace to attract attention. But at all times avoid a snail's pace; along with being dubbed a slow thinker, you may also be labeled dull. Occasional brief pauses are all right, but keep the pauses silent. Don't fill the space with "uh" or nervously clear your throat.

How to Improve the Way You Sound

Whether you need to work on your tone, articulation, pitch, volume, energy and enthusiasm, rhythm, or pace, the following tips will help.

▪ Review the answers you gave to the quiz at the beginning of the chapter. With those answers in mind, speak into a tape recorder and listen to how you really handle tone, articulation, pitch, volume, energy and enthusiasm, rhythm, and pace. To get a true sample of your speech patterns, keep the recorder by your telephone and record one day's calls.

▪ Ask a friend or co-worker to give you honest feedback. Have that person evaluate you on the foregoing specifics.

▪ Make a list of the sounds you use repeatedly to fill in gaps and silences. Work to eliminate these fillers.

▪ Work on voice exercises. Your public library will have books on voice improvement, with exercises for practice. Four suggested titles are: *Speak Like a Pro: In Business and Public Speaking,* by Margaret Bedrosian; *Speech Can Change Your Life,* by Dorothy Sarnoff; and *The Secret of Charisma: What It Is and How to Get It,* by Doe Lang. There are audio- and videocassettes on voice improvement and effective communication, too. Your local library may have some you can borrow. If not, it may have information on where cassettes are available in your area.

▪ Take a course in public speaking. Many evening courses are taught in high school adult-education classes or college continuing-education departments. Another possibility is to join an organization such as International Training In Communication (P.O. Box 4249, Anaheim, California 92803) or your local Toastmasters Public Speaking Club (in telephone book), or write Toastmasters International World Headquarters, 2200 North Grand Avenue, P.O. Box 10400, Santa Ana, California 92711.

▪ Consult a speech specialist. You'll find specialists listed in the yellow pages of many phone books under "Speech Improvement—Voice and Diction." If you don't find any leads in your phone book, a call or letter directed to the head of the speech department of an area college may yield references. While you're looking for a specialist (or a speech course), however, select one that uses videotapes. As speech specialist Sandy Linver points out, seeing yourself on video is the best possible way to get outside of yourself and see and hear what others actually see and hear.

CHAPTER 3

Choose Your Words Carefully

"I felt that acting responsibly and quickly was the best decision for the company."

A large part of getting your verbal messages across depends on selecting words and phrases that help, rather than handicap, your efforts to obtain the responses you want. Thus, people with high verbal IQs avoid expressions that trigger defensive responses and, instead, season their talk with words and phrases that make listeners respond positively to what they are saying.

The words that you use to convey thoughts or intentions come packaged with auxiliary meanings, too, so you'll reinforce your professional image and strengthen your verbal personality if you monitor your use of words. Certain words and expressions can be verbal buffers that prevent conversational collisions while increasing your visibility in corporate confrontations.

Sometimes called soft phrases, these verbal buffers are effective lead-ins for stating your point of view, defending a position, or easing away from an angry reply.

To be effective, verbal buffers must show your respect for and interest in the person or persons with whom you are speaking. "The first words that come out of your mouth should indicate that you have heard, understood, and appreciated the other person's position," says Dr. Paula Kurman, industry consultant and director of Communicational Judo, Inc. According to Kurman, this means your speech should not be couched in clichés that contain advice, instructions, opinions, or judgments. Instead, the words you use should fit the context of the conversation.

For example, suppose you've assigned a new task to one of your workers and you get this angry response: "How can you expect me to do that, too? My desk is already an avalanche of paper. I have so many things to do I don't have time to breathe."

PAT RESPONSE (advice): "Here's what you should do, then. Make a list of your priorities and chip away at them one at a time."

RELEVANT RESPONSE: "I understand how you feel about your work load, and I know that when you have so much to do this extra request can seem overwhelming. But. . . ."

"The second response," continues Kurman, "indicates that you've heard, understood, and appreciated. You've responded empathetically to what the other person said."

Five Categories of Winning Words

There are five types of soft phrases you can use to indicate that you've heard, understood, and appreciated the other person's position.

1. *Words that tranquilize and pacify.* When you're on the *giving* end of orders and reprimands, you can use tranquilizing phrases to encourage a calm, controlled atmosphere.

23

Don, a manager in the employee benefits department of a corporation, noticed that Glen, a junior member of his staff, omitted certain information from a presentation on the company's early retirement plan. Don handled the situation ineptly. Without first thinking about his choice of words, he said to Glen angrily, "Where's the early retirement plan? We discussed that, don't you remember?" Stung by those words, Glen fought back. After a hot and heavy exchange, their meeting ended with an impasse, neither Don or Glen knowing what to do next.

Instead of being so harsh and backing Glen against the wall, Don could have first asked if there was a reason for the omission. As Marc Dorio, vice-president of an international management consulting firm, suggests, "For example, he might have said 'Glen, I notice that in this presentation there's nothing about the early retirement program we discussed. Did you have any reason for this?' In that way Don, as manager, could have *given* Glen an out and a chance to do something about the problem."

When you use words to tranquilize and pacify, you don't abandon your values or surrender your position. But in many cases, you do prevent a strained situation from becoming an outright conflict. Here are some verbal buffers to lessen the impact of a conversational collision when you give reprimands:

"It would seem that you. . . ."

"It was my impression that. . . ."

"It was my understanding that we. . . ."

"Let's talk this over so we can. . . ."

"It might be possible to manage. . . ."

2. *Words that ease confrontations and conflicts.* When you're on the *receiving* end of reprimands, you can use words to ease confrontations. For example, in an episode similar to the previous one, Joan, an actuarial assistant, was the *receiver* of harsh words. Stan, the president of the actuarial firm, exploded when he learned that Joan had mailed some papers to a client at

the client's request. "Why the hell didn't you get my approval to send the material out?" he demanded when he called Joan into his office.

Joan, however, kept her cool. Unlike Glen, who lost control, Joan told Stan in a calm manner that she felt the request was so urgent it was critical to get the material out as quickly as possible in order to keep the client. When she had a chance to explain why she thought it was so urgent, she said to Stan, "It was my immediate feeling that the papers had to be mailed at once, and that if we delayed, they would arrive too late to be of use to the client. I felt that acting swiftly was the best decision for the company, so it was my intention to be responsible and efficient."

Here are some words and phrases to help ease confrontations and conflicts:

"Let me explain. . . ."

"It's possible you might agree with me when. . . ."

"Let's look at what we can do to remedy this. . . ."

"I know you're upset, and I'm sorry. But I'd like a chance to work this out. . . ."

3. *Words that convey a sense of urgency.* Most people don't have a sense of urgency in their language, so you stand out when you do. This is pointed out by Marc Dorio, who uses the example of two managers asked by their boss, "Has the report gone to Cleveland?"

Dorio explains, "In both cases the managers' secretaries were typing the report at the time the boss asked the question. Since that was the case, manager 1 answered, 'No, it hasn't gone out yet.' Manager 2, however, sensed the urgency in his boss's question and matched it with his own urgency by replying reassuredly, 'We are working on it. Consider it done.' Then he asked his secretary if anything could be done to speed it through."

In another situation, a customer phoned a manager and

asked, "Are my goods being delivered?" Manager 1, who had people working on the order in the warehouse, answered, "We're working on your order now. I hope to get it out today." But manager 2 spoke up and said, again reassuredly, "Don't worry about it. It's being taken care of as we speak. Your order is on the way."

By the end of the day, both the report to Cleveland and the customer's order were sent out. But in each case, manager 2's trigger-word reply was a stronger reply, which provided greater satisfaction to the person receiving the response while ultimately enhancing the manager's image.

"Using words that convey a sense of urgency comes out of that all-important empathetic reflection of another person's need," stresses Paula Kurman. "When you underline your appreciation of the other's person's urgency with, 'I can see this matter is very important,' the other person relaxes because he has heard that you understand this is top priority." Kurman further points out that acknowledging the importance of the situation is more critical than the remainder of your response.

Here are some words and phrases to help you convey a sense of urgency:

"I'll get right on it."

"I'll do it immediately."

"I'll have it for you today."

"Don't worry. I'll take care of it."

"I can see this matter is very important."

4. *Words that help you defend yourself (when you must).* You'll note "when you must" is tacked on to this category. This is because there are some situations when defending yourself is pointless, and if there's a hole in your defense, you'll just provoke another attack. But there are times when you are in the right and it is advantageous to speak up for yourself. At those times you have to be prepared to defend yourself with the right words.

"Show your command of your subject succinctly and per-suasively," advises Mark Clemente, a marketing director for an accounting and management consulting firm. "But don't lock yourself in, since there are many cases where there's no right or wrong. You have to be flexible in terms of giving your supervisors what they say they want. If you had good reason for your decision or action, pointing out that reason can often show your intuition and sensitivity even though the action or decision might have been wrong."

Here are some words and phrases to help you defend yourself:

"It was my feeling. . . ."

"I hope you will understand. . . ."

"It would seem that taking that action was best."

"Here is the way I thought it should be done, and here is my reason for doing it this way."

"There are still other things we can try."

5. *Words that translate into the framework of other people's reality and understanding.* "Let me set you straight," "Let me clue you in," and "Let me give you a tip or two" are irritating and condescending if said in superior ways. Along with overly general phrases, they're also useless because they can't be translated to reach other people's reality and understanding.

In talking about relating your words to other people's sense of reality and understanding, Paula Kurman cites the example of a company troubled by interdepartmental strife. "Let's say that, in a very general way, a manager in the human resources department is trying to educate a manager in the finance department on the human element of business. During their conversation the human resources manager says to the finance manager, 'You don't care about people.'

"In using that approach, the manager from human resources is not translating what he wants to say into a metaphor

27

the manager in finance can understand, so the words are a wasted effort. To be more effective, the human resources manager might say, 'I'd like to show you some facts and figures that relate to our personnel policies.' "

Here are some other words and phrases from the example of the human resources manager and the manager in finance that show you how to couch words in terms of other people's framework of reality and understanding. These can be adapted to your own business situation:

"I appreciate your need to hold down costs but. . . ."

"I understand your thinking in not wanting to appropriate money for raises across the board, but to keep our employees happy could we agree to? . . ."

"Let's review our present salary structure together and talk about. . . ."

"I sympathize with your position that low profitability will affect bonuses, but let's try to give everyone a piece of the pie—or else give no bonuses at all."

Words and Phrases to Avoid

At the opposite end of the spectrum from the five categories of winning words and phrases are four categories of ineffective ones you'll do well to forgo.

1. *Extraneous expressions.* There are meaningless expressions that people often toss into their conversation out of habit. Avoid using the following words at the beginning, middle, and end of your sentences:

- *Like*—Often thrown in as though it were a pause. "We were like going to do that tomorrow."

28

- *Right?*—Tacked on to the end of a sentence, as if insecure. "It was a good meeting, right?"
- *You understand?*—Added to emphasize a point. "That report should be compressed to a page and a half, you understand?"
- *You know*—Thrown in at the end or beginning of a sentence, as a space filler. "John is a good team member, you know."

2. *Pointless, routine statements.* The following are hackneyed expressions that serve no function in verbal communication. They do little for your verbal image, so drop them from your speech:

- *Sort of*—It's ambiguous and clarifies nothing.
- *More or less*—It says nothing.
- *I guess*—It shows lack of strength or conviction.
- *And so forth*—Too often a shield for not having full information.
- *If you know what I mean*—Managers are supposed to say what they mean, without having to qualify their words.
- *I know you won't believe this*—If you don't think people will believe your words, choose ones that are convincing.
- *What I'm really trying to say is*—Don't just try to say it. Think through your words and then say what you mean.

3. *Abrasive words and phrases.* Harsh, shouting responses shut down the lines of communication as soon as you say the words. The following expressions are so offensive none needs an explanation:

"You don't understand."

"Of course I'm right."

"Do it my way!"

"What is it you're driving at?"

"You're wrong!"

"What kind of suggestion is that?"

"Who would want to use your idea?"

4. *Pass-the-buck words.* It's human nature to want to blame others when you're criticized for something. But passing the buck is self-damaging and irritating to the person who has to listen to your excuses.

"Whatever the mess-up is, blaming others doesn't help. The person who gets ahead is the one who asks, 'What can I do now?' 'How can we fix it?' 'What is the next step to make this better?' " explains Paula Kurman. "But unfortunately some people don't understand when they blame others they portray themselves as a victim and put themselves in a weak and helpless position rather than a position of strength.

"In many cases, biting your tongue and accepting responsibility works out better than passing the buck with 'It's not my fault. I was waiting for Fred to give it to me and he was late this morning,' " continues Kurman. "Admittedly, this can be hard to accept for people who have spent their lives feeling that somehow, if something is their fault, they are less of a person. But actually, taking responsibility makes them *more* of a person." Kurman reminds us of the famous sign on Harry Truman's desk: THE BUCK STOPS HERE.

Mark Clemente agrees that if there's a problem, a manager needs to communicate the fact that she is trying to find the solution immediately. Advises Clemente, "If you're in the right, you can preface your approach with 'I beg to differ, but here's the situation, here's what I was assigned to do, and here's what I did. If that was ——'s responsibility, I'm not sure how he handled it or whether he did handle it. But if it's messed up, that's the reality, and there's a problem regardless of whose fault it is. How can we solve it and how can I help?' When you approach it that way," concludes Clemente, "you hit the ball back to the person who's confronting you."

Polish Your Verbal Skills

Here are four rules to keep in mind as you work on developing your verbal IQ through better word choice.

1. *Speak correctly*. Obviously, if you want to strengthen your upper-management potential, you must watch your use of the English language. Pay close attention to grammar and usage. For example, in the space of one week I heard managers use the following wrong constructions:

WRONG	RIGHT
I seen him on the elevator.	I saw him on the elevator.
It should have been him giving that report.	He should have given that report.
She come to my office.	She came to my office.
He says to me.	He said to me.
There was two people there.	There were two people there.
We was in Chicago together.	We were in Chicago together.
The order was given to Jane and I.	The order was given to Jane and me.
She goes "I went out to lunch with Clyde."	She said, "I went out to lunch with Clyde."
It's me.	It's I.
I could of done that.	I could have done that.

That's only a smattering of the phrases that can put you in a bad grammatical light. If you feel insecure about your grammar, or if you've grown careless with it, brush up a bit with a grammar handbook.

The classic book for this is *The Elements of Style,* written by Cornell University professor William Strunk, Jr. It was first published in 1918, and has been revised twice by Dr. Strunk's former student, renowned writer E. B. White. It is considered a bible for basic grammar and usage.

Another practical book is *Write Right,* by Jan Venolia. In addition, many adult schools, community colleges, and adult learning centers give refresher courses in grammar. Make a few phone calls to determine what's available in your area.

2. *Give the right "I don't know" response.* A good verbal image can never be built on an "I don't know" attitude. If someone asks a question and you don't know the answer, admit it, but don't leave it at that. You'll make a far better impression if you respond with:

"I don't know, but I'll find out."

"I'll do what it takes to get that answer."

"I'll take care of getting the answer."

"I'll find out that information."

"Give me a chance to get back to you with that."

These phrases can see you through many encounters when a brief "I don't know" would be damaging to your image.

There are many situations when an admission of ignorance doesn't mean you're stupid. For example, Paula Kurman recalls an academic meeting at which she saw everyone looking very professorial while the person leading the meeting was using acronyms to refer to groups and programs without explaining their meaning. "The initials were alphabet soup in my mind. Yet when I looked around, everyone was nodding in assent. It seemed to me that I was the only person there who didn't know what was going on."

Unafraid of admitting her ignorance, Kurman made a list of the abbreviations and then raised her hand and said, "Excuse me for interrupting, but I really don't know what you're talking about when you use some of those initials. If you'll just tell me what the following stand for, I'll write them down on this paper. Then I'll simply refer to my list and not bother you again."

"The leader was very gracious," Kurman recalls. "Moreover, when the meeting was over, the person sitting next to me thanked me for asking for that information and admitted that he, too, had no idea what the initials meant." As Kurman illustrates, it's not always a bad thing to be uninformed, but it *is* bad not to do something about it.

3. *Use opening and closing conversation.* Depending upon the situation, a good opener can generally get communication going, whether the meeting is with a new contact or a person with whom you work side by side. Obviously, if it's a first encounter, you can open with "Hello, my name is. . . ." *Always* use your full name because just a first name is too informal for business and shows a lack of respect.

After the introduction, continue with a phrase that indicates your interest in the other person and shifts attention away from you. For example:

"Tell me what you're doing."

"How's your project going?"

"What can I do for you today?"

This gets the encounter off to a good start. When the discussion is finished, you need to close with an equally friendly expression. For instance:

"Thanks to your help and suggestions we're off to a good start."

"This discussion has been most productive, and we've done what we needed to do today."

"I look forward to our next meeting and will soon be calling you about it."

By ending in this positive way rather than merely fading away, you (1) sum up what has been accomplished, (2) indicate whether or not the business at hand is ended, (3) clarify whether there will be a follow-up meeting, and (4) keep the door open for future business, whatever that might be.

4. *Develop your own style.* Sound like yourself when you talk. As long as you keep it within reasonable confines, your speech is part of your personality and it belongs to you.

Although, as we previously pointed out, it's important to speak correctly and abide by the rules of basic grammar, there are exceptions to every rule. The exception here is the appropriate use of regional expressions that—when they come naturally to you—heighten your verbal IQ and enhance your speaking style by putting your best words forward in a way that's distinctively your own.

Harry Truman, for instance, took many of his Missouri small-town phrases to Washington. Few people will forget his way of referring to the White House lawn as the front yard. Likewise, a prominent director of research for a large pharmaceutical house was educated at the finest colleges. But his regional heritage was Vermont farm country, so it was natural that he use the fractured words and phrases of his childhood. Because of his professional acumen, his company sent him all over the world, and wherever he went those regional expressions gave his speech its special flavor.

A Final Checklist

1. Make a list of extraneous words and phrases you find yourself using repeatedly. Refer to it often to remind yourself to avoid them.
2. Use peoples' names in your conversations; there is nothing more flattering.
3. Pronounce people's names properly. It isn't flattering to mispronounce names, so if people's names are difficult, learn the correct pronunciation and practice it. (It's *never* funny to joke about a name.)

4. Use simple words. Avoid words that are too long; they will not impress the other person.
5. Only use a word when you know its meaning.
6. Be concise. Don't talk so much that you bury your point in irrelevant details.

CHAPTER 4

Wait for Your Cue

"Tell me more about it."

Listening to what others say is vital to your management career, since companies need good listeners as well as good problem solvers. Yet if you're like most people, you listen and comprehend at only 25 percent of your ability—even though managers reportedly spend 60 to 75 percent of their time gathering information by listening to others.

Consider these familiar scenarios: You ask someone a question, then only half-listen to the answer. You pretend to listen while you daydream or concentrate on your own thoughts. You avoid eye contact with someone speaking to you and you let your eyes wander to other conversations and distractions. You tap your foot, look at your watch, and reveal that you are bored while you wait for someone to finish so you can start talking yourself.

Philosopher, professor, and author Dr. Mortimer Adler gives this example of a conversation between hypothetical characters Smith and Brown:

Smith speaks and Brown appears to be listening, but in reality Brown is thinking of what he's going to say when Smith stops talking. Smith is now quiet and Brown says what is on his mind—

36

even though it may have nothing to do with what Smith has just said. Meanwhile Smith is thinking of what he's going to say next. Their conversation is like two ships that pass in the night, with no signals exchanged.[1]

The Untaught Skill

Though most managers have received formal training in reading, writing, and speaking, few have been taught to listen—often referred to as the untaught skill. Many managers listen poorly, despite the fact that research and studies by communication experts have shown that people spend far more time listening than reading, writing, or talking. And even though listening is only one part of verbal communication (and not a means of communication itself), good listening ability has been found to be central to most people's personal, social, educational, and professional success.

Because one of the primary needs of people in business is to be heard, how skilled you are at listening can have a tremendous effect on your upper-management potential. Gay A. Mayer, president and CEO of MEM Company, has stressed this factor in successful management: "Learn how to listen. You've got to hear grass growing, got to understand what people are telling you, even if it isn't obvious. People appreciate being heard. Everyone wants his day in court."[2]

Managers Need Listening Skills

In addition to bolstering your business relationships and encouraging your professional growth, knowing how and when to listen can achieve the following:

1. Clarify misunderstandings and diffuse potential conflicts.
2. Prevent mistakes and save money.

3. Provide ways to analyze people with whom you do business and give you feedback on their interests.
4. Make others more receptive to a different viewpoint (people are more apt to listen to you if you have listened to them and understand their views).
5. Help you expand your management ability as you ask "How can I use this information?" "Where will it work for me?" and "How can I apply it to help someone else?"

Just as effective listening has strong positive results, ineffective listening can produce some powerful negatives:

1. Intensify crises and conflicts.
2. Cause you to miss or lose important information.
3. Result in frustration, injured self-esteem, embarrassment, and confusion.
4. Weaken your personal relationships.
5. Bring about unnecessary financial losses (even the smallest listening errors such as letters that have to be retyped and appointments that need rescheduling can cost business many dollars).

Consider this example of how poor listening habits cost a promising assistant her job. Bruce, a magazine fiction editor, hired an assistant, Jane, who, while being trained, also served as his secretary and had heavy typing duties. Jane had taken the assistant's job because she felt it would pave the way to becoming an editor. But she hated her typing duties and felt they were beneath her.

Jane was so intent on absorbing editorial knowledge that she never listened to what her boss asked her to say in letters and manuscript reports. Along with not knowing how to listen, Jane was so confident of her own judgment that she typed what she thought should be right without listening to the directions that were given her. As a result, much of her work had to be redone to reflect what Bruce wanted to say. Bruce tolerated this for several months, but finally let Jane go, despite her editorial potential.

Don Christman, a training consultant for the banking and financial services industry, and author of a chapter on effective listening in the *Handbook of Engineering Management,* divides the results of poor listening into two groups: personal effects and organizational effects. According to Christman:

> A prime personal effect on managers is an impaired ability to interpret accurately and implement verbally communicative directives from higher management. Other effects are impaired ability to benefit maximally from staff input received in one-on-one dialogues, decreased sensitivity in interpersonal dialogue with subordinates, and less awareness of actual or potential problems concerning attitude and morale.[3]

In discussing the effects of poor listening on the organization, Christman pinpoints "feedback problems resulting from instructions and directives, inefficient supervision of project development, lost time through lapses in communciation with subordinates, impairment of inner-departmental coordination due to lack of understanding or misunderstandings, compromised awareness of project and personnel problems as they arise, and company-wide productivity penalty caused by effect on work flow of performance and morale problems."[4]

Are You a Poor Listener?

A major reason why some managers are poor listeners is that listening is a learned behavior and few of us have mastered it. Consequently, many managers communicate in monologues rather than dialogues. Christman attributes this to three basic reasons:

1. Habit—it's a characteristic we have carried since child-hood.

2. Inclination—it's an ego matter, natural proclivity that interferes with our ability to listen; we're more interested in our own words than in other people's words.
3. Lack of listening tools—we haven't learned how to listen.

Fortunately, the last item is a shortcoming that managers can correct with a focused and directed effort.

Listening experts and trainers say that most people make more than one listening mistake every day, including the four in the scenarios cited at the start of this chapter. Starting with those four, here are the twelve most common listening mistakes:

1. Asking someone a question and only half-listening to the answer
2. Pretending to listen while daydreaming or concentrating on your own thoughts
3. Avoiding eye contact with someone speaking to you and letting your eyes wander to other conversations and distractions
4. Tapping your foot, looking at your watch, and revealing that you are bored while you wait for others to finish so you can start talking yourself
5. Ignoring other people's views because, even though you hear the words, you don't make the effort to evaluate and understand their message or be sensitive to their feelings and emotions
6. Jumping to conclusions and being too quick to call something dull, uninteresting, and unimportant
7. Offering unasked for solutions and not realizing that many people would rather have you listen than give advice
8. Being preoccupied with your own job and your personal pressures
9. Misinterpreting what people say because of precon-

ceived notions, expectations, experiences, and perspectives
10. Deciding automatically that something is "over your head"
11. Judging a person's words on their delivery rather than their content
12. Engaging in passive rather than active listening

Be an Active Listener

Too often, we make listening a passive process, rather than an active one. But active listening is of prime importance for a high verbal IQ. Managers must put passivity behind them and become actively concerned when others speak. You should listen with your eyes, ears, and heart—and respond when the time is right. Mortimer Adler sums it up:

Unless your mind as well as your ear is involved you aren't really listening. Your job is to reach out and catch what is in the mind of the speaker—just as the catcher in a baseball game must actively stretch for the ball the pitcher has just thrown.

A good listener is not distracted by the speaker's mannerisms or tone of voice. You must try to understand the intentions of the speaker. What is he really trying to tell you? If you are not sure you've understood, there's a simple technique that you can use. Say "Did I understand you to say—" (and put what you think the other person has said in your own words). If the speaker agrees you've stated the point correctly, then you are free to agree or disagree.[5]

Put Your Listening Skills to Work

Many managers wonder if appearing to accept what others say (temporarily, at least) will be interpreted as agreement. Bury your fears, however, because understanding another person's point of view and acknowledging its importance are not the same as agreeing with it. *Understanding* is the key word here; as Dr. Adler has explained, "To agree before you understand what the other person has said is inane. To disagree before you understand is impertinent."[6]

Another concern many managers have is when to shift the listening role back to the other person and when to give that person a chance to speak. This sense of when to speak and when to listen is a verbal communication skill that develops only with practice. But while you're honing and refining it, you'll do well to lean more toward keeping quiet. Spend more time listening to others before you respond. This is especially true when dealing with difficult co-workers—complainers, for example, who try your patience but whose opinions need adequate time to be heard.

In one such case, Michael, an assistant manager in a department store (and a person who'd always been good on the job), was burdened with wall-to-wall problems at home, including a father in a nursing home whom he had to visit each week, an errant son in trouble with the law, and a wife who wanted a divorce. As Michael faced these problems at home, each crisis at work overwhelmed him, so he became a complainer about almost everything.

Fortunately for Michael, his boss, Janet, was sensitive to Michael's atypical behavior. Until his domestic problems were solved, she kept quiet and listened to his complaints. And at the same time that response was helpful to Michael, it earned respect for Janet from her supervisors.

With a little effort, you can make good listening part of your verbal communication skills. Christman suggests the following three things.

First, organize what people are saying, as you go along, in terms of the key words they use while speaking. The key words will be the action words that pinpoint an area of meaning in their message. Focus on these key words and memorize them, so you can recall the substance and content of the conversation.

Second, make a conscious decision to filter out emotion, bias, irrelevancy, redundancy, background noise and distractions, and peculiarities of speech or foreign accents. If someone has an unusual accent, many people get focused on that and don't hear what the person has said. By screening out these distractions you can focus on key words and content.

Third, develop the ability to separate the speaker's content into primary and secondary points.

Remember the primary points by means of key words. The secondary points usually flow from these.

As an example, Daniel, a district manager for a food service company, learned from his regional manager that X Corporation (with whom Daniel's company had contracts for running its cafeterias) would not be renewing its contract. X Corporation had several divisions with separate cafeterias in each, so Daniel had to visit each division to advise the cafeteria managers that since the company was losing the contract, the food service staff would be out of a job.

When he met the managers, his message to each one was: "We didn't want this to happen, but X Corporation is not renewing its food service contract with us. December 31 will be our last day in this cafeteria. Let your staff members know this cutoff date so that they can look for jobs while they are still employed here."

In this situation "not renewing food service contract" is obviously the primary point because it pinpoints the problem. The secondary points would be "December 31 last day," "let staff members know," and "look for jobs."

Most of the managers listened and comprehended Daniel's message. But, as usual, there was a manager so preoccupied with other matters be heard only the primary point and had to phone Daniel the following day to obtain the other details. "When did you say we were closing down?" the manager asked. "What should I tell my people? Will the company place us somewhere else, or will we be out of a job?"

Experts in listening conclude that, like this cafeteria manager, many people exhibit poor listening skills every day. Cut

43

down on this in your own management career by keeping these additional pointers in mind.

1. Listen to people's names and use them.
2. Let speakers finish their sentences before you interrupt or try to change the subject.
3. Ask questions to see if your interpretations of what other people say are correct.
4. Indicate you're listening by giving belief comments such as "I see," "I understand," "That must have been a great experience," "Your response is appropriate," and "Tell me more about it."
5. Develop a sensitivity for what is left unsaid and for the inner feelings words often mask.

Finally, keep sharpening your listening skills by reading and studying books on the subject. (See "For Further Reading" for recommended titles.) There are also video series and audiocassettes available from libraries, bookstores, and audio/video centers.

PART II

Put Your Best Words Forward

CHAPTER 5

The Information You Need

"I have a problem I'd like to discuss with you."

"Knowledge is of two kinds: we know a subject ourselves, or we know where we can find information upon it," said Samuel Johnson at the end of the eighteenth century. This is still apropos because getting information from key personnel, finding out what others need and think, and tapping into the office grapevine give managers insight and perspective, which ultimately help them chart their career.

By every standard, the managers who get ahead are those who place a high value on knowing what goes on in both their company and the industry. And, happily, in most organizations there are persons—fonts of information—who always seem aware of what's important to know. These valued sources form a support system all managers need.

So how do you use your verbal skills to become part of this system? How do you set up an information network? And while you seek information how do you use your verbal performance to show your upper-management potential? This chapter presents six strategies for getting more information and using it to enhance your potential.

Strategy 1. Identify Your Best Sources

As all managers know, an organization has two power structures: the visible one that's detailed on the organizational chart and the invisible one composed of the real movers and shakers.

Before you can set up an information network of your best sources, study the organizational chart and personnel manual for about half an hour. Then think about the invisible power structure—the key managers and others who really have the power.

Henry C. Rogers, author of *Rogers' Rules for Business-women,* defines the power structure as "the key people who get things done, who execute policy and who make critical decisions."[1] They are not necessarily those in top management, but are often people who are moving up rapidly and who predictably will be the top management of tomorrow.

An influential person, points out Marc Dorio, vice-president of an international management consulting firm, "could be the boss's secretary because, if she doesn't like you and doesn't perceive you to be an ally, you're dead before you even get started."

To determine who the influential people are—and how they can affect your career—answer the following questions:

1. Who does what job and where?
2. Which people have the most influence and prestige?
3. Who spends time with the top brass and seems to communicate with them most often?
4. Who has made significant upward progress?
5. Which managers answer questions from insiders and outsiders without having to get help from others?

6. Who is always being quoted?
7. Which people are frequently consulted by other managers and specialists?
8. Who makes important and responsible decisions—and why?
9. Who writes the major memos?
10. Who chairs meetings and makes important announcements?
11. Which of these people can help you reach your goals?
12. What do those persons know that you need to know?

Strategy 2. Expand Your Contacts

After you identify the key people, there are four steps to setting up your information network.

1. *Cultivate your relationships with key people.* Begin small, with just one supportive person, if necessary, and build slowly to a full network.

"You have to establish allies and reach out to the company's top persons in order to find out what's going on and what people are doing and thinking," stresses Doe Lang, president and founder of the Manhattan-based Charismedia Services for Comfortable Effective Speaking.

"It's in every manager's best interest to find out what the top people's issues and expertise are," says Laura Hart, press aide to Manhattan Borough President David N. Dinkins. "Then you can tap into many different issues and become involved in them."

In order to cultivate relationships and tap into issues and knowledge, get to your office early and invite people in for some coffee and Danish (or a special "goody" you bring from home), relax together over drinks after work, or get involved with key people in company-sponsored social and recreational events.

"There's no way a manager can work in a vacuum and be a

one-issue type of person," continues Hart, whose high-pressure job involves her in many city government issues.

2. *Become informed.* Research the background of your organization's key people. Keep up with what is going on in the industry. Have information at your fingertips to pass on to important people. For example, read the business section of your major newspaper; also read the business magazines and trade journals. Be sure to see your company's annual report, and request and read copies of speeches, newsletters, press releases, memos from top executives, and anything else the people at the top are reading.

In addition, Don Bagin, publisher of the nationally distributed newsletter *communication briefings,* advises the manager to "cite trends that could have an impact on your organization. By being recognized as one who reads in the field and can identify directions that the company should pursue you will be seen as an important colleague."[2]

You'll be viewed, adds Bagin, as an overall manager rather than someone with a narrow area of responsibility. He suggests you say to your boss, "Here's an article I've clipped that relates to. . . ." Or, "In my reading I've noticed this new trend that shows the direction some companies are taking."

You can also obtain information by getting on the routing slips for important periodicals, journals, and reports. Many periodicals are circulated around the company.

Show that you're anxious to keep on top of information by asking to see these periodicals. Then, when the material comes to you, notice which periodicals and journals go to the offices of influential people—and include those publications in your reading matter.

When possible, ask for copies of reports not routinely distributed. When you hear that a certain report has been completed and think you could benefit from it, borrow or obtain a copy—ideally from a top person so your interest will be visible.

3. *Join the important business and professional organizations.* Find out which organizations the key executives in your

company belong to. This helps you solidify contacts while also keeping you abreast of the latest happenings in your industry.

Ask questions and make comments at the meetings. When you do this effectively and express yourself well, others will look your way. Similarly, volunteer to serve on committees that give you access to top managers. And circulate as much as you can, speaking up with phrases such as:

"Is there any way I can help?"

"I'd like a chance to work with you."

"How's your project going?"

"Tell me what you're doing."

"I have a problem I'd like to discuss with you."

"You deserve a compliment for how you moderated that panel."

4. *Make additional contacts through networking groups.* As a member of one or more networks, you can trade business cards, information, advice, and referrals with other managers. A good source for locating such groups is *Networking: The First Report and Directory,* by Jessica Lipnack and Jeffrey Stamps.

Strategy 3. Show You Are Interested in Them

Find out what the special interests are of key people. One excellent way to do this, as Henry C. Rogers points out in his book *Rogers' Rules for Businesswomen,* is to note what your co-workers and boss talk about most.

Is it management issues? Production problems? Customer relations? New business opportunities? Increased efficiency? Politics? New films? Real estate?

Whatever they talk about you should become as knowledgeable about these subjects as any one in the company. Then you'll feel comfortable participating in conversations with clients and colleagues.[3]

Once you know their interests, clip and pass on any articles or items that relate to their interests. This need not be limited to business interests. When appropriate, it is refreshing to keep other pursuits in mind.

"Anytime I see an article on someone's specific area of interest—say, sailing—I make a copy of the article and send it along with a note saying 'For your information—hope this can be of help,'" says Milo Sobel, a management educator and expert in communication. "This is a way of keeping in contact with people without calling them only when you need information. There's nothing worse than that. But when you've been sending them notes on their special interest, you can call them when you need something. They'll remember that you were the person who sent them clippings, and probably will say 'What can I do for you?'"

As you discover people's interests and passions, set up a reference file to keep track of them. Talk about those interests when you're with those people. So you won't forget what you've talked about, take notes as soon as possible afterwards. Keep the file up-to-date and add to it when you have new information.

Strategy 4. Get People to Talk

If you can encourage people to talk, they will give you more information and ultimately be impressed with you. Obviously, one way to accomplish this is to build on their special interests by making their priorities your priorities. A second way is to become a good listener, as pointed out in Chapter 4.

A third way to get people to talk is to approach them when they're relaxed and unhurried. Rather than interrupting someone at an untoward time, approach the person with something like:

"I'd like a chance to talk with you."

"What's the best time for us to talk about something?"

"I need to find out———, and I'd like to draw on your knowledge, when it's convenient for you."

A fourth way to encourage someone to talk is to be direct and to the point. As the last sentence in the above list indicates, rather than beating around the bush, tell the person exactly what information you want and why you want or need it. This directness will sometimes prompt someone to talk, since he or she is flattered to be thought of as a knowledgeable individual.

A fifth way is to be friendly, interested, and open. When you ask for information in this manner, people are more apt to cooperate and communicate with you. But don't be so friendly that you appear false. "Your style or manner can't be phoney," warns Laura Hart. "You have to have a genuine interest in people that goes beyond being friendly and interested just for the sake of appearing friendly and interested.

"Humor goes a long way, too," Hart continues, in explaining a sixth way to get people to talk. "You can encourage people to open up by lightening up situations and making appropriate humorous observations at appropriate times. Former President Ronald Reagan, for instance, was known for his ability to quip and find humor in the most difficult situation."

Strategy 5. Gain People's Trust

Trust is based on honesty and integrity. As you attach yourself to people who can give you information and help your professional growth, you build that trust by showing interest in that person and her work, by asking intelligent questions, by working hard and thoroughly, and by demonstrating your willingness to learn. But your efforts have to be genuine because, as noted, you can't play up to others for self-serving information.

For example, Skip, a branch manager in a large travel agency, appeared to be everyone's buddy as he mingled not only within his own agency but also throughout the industry. As time went on, however, Skip's jovial backslapping and verbal communication became highly questionable. His colleagues discovered, one by one, that Skip's only interest in talking with them was to pump them for information that he could use to his own advantage—to the point of stealing their clients from them. Soon all of his colleagues shunned him and zipped their mouths shut whenever they saw him approach.

"If you are saying one thing to be nice and part of you is thinking something else, that latter part will show—and people will not trust you," said Dr. Paula Kurman, director of Communicational Judo, Inc.

"Hidden agendas are always wrong. Coming right out and laying on the table exactly what it is you want is always a far better idea than self-serving negatives, as long as the other person's needs are taken into account also. When all of you is giving off the same message simultaneously, you can be trusted."

"And when you're trusted," adds Laura Hart, "you can be taken into the fold without fear that you're attaching yourself for an insidious reason."

In addition, you can gain and build people's trust by doing the following:

1. Be discreet. Know when it's all right to pass on information and when you should keep it to yourself so people can rely on you.
2. Protect your source when a confidence is requested. No matter how much you are pressured, refuse to identify your sources.
3. Unless you can't appropriately identify the source, credit

people for the ideas they pass on, rather than acting as though the ideas were yours.

Strategy 6. Share Your Knowledge

Gathering information is a two-way street. If you want others to channel information to you, you have to be prepared to share your knowledge, too. Occasionally, we have had negative experiences when we've been generous with our information. But we learn from these negative experiences and become more savvy about when and where—and with whom—to share. There's no real reason to feel threatened.

"In my case, I try to make every effort to help when people have questions," reports Laura Hart. "Unsolicited, I won't go in and do this. But if I'm queried, I'll share my experiences and suggest approaches people might take. This kind of sharing can benefit the person who shares it, too, because at the same time as you're helping someone else, you're helping yourself articulate and understand what you're doing."

"The more things you generously do for people, the more people are going to want to do for you," adds Doe Lang. "You may not always get credit. But if you're the kind of person who does good things for other people, you become known as a resource—someone who can be counted on for good ideas and good feelings, and to whom people go for support and encouragement. That aura begins to spread and people start to know about it."

As you gain visibility by helping others, it's smart to help your boss succeed, too. According to most managers, the old saw—that you look good if you make your boss look good—is as true as ever. Moreover, as Don Bagin explains, by helping your boss look good, you enhance the chance that he or she will be promoted—and that can have positive ramifications for you, too.[4]

Use Information to Increase Your Visibility

By identifying your best resources, expanding your contacts, getting others to talk, gaining people's trust, and sharing your knowledge, you can increase your visibility and publicize your aspirations and accomplishments.

"I believe in doing this kind of personal public relations for yourself," advises Michael Levine, a prominent publicist who represents such entertainment stars as Mickey Rooney, Charlton Heston, and Linda Evans. "Most people in the workplace are invisible and known to only a small network or group of people. This is a long way from the high visibility earned by people in much more prominent positions. But, whereas fifty years ago there were only movie stars who were publicized celebrities, today there are politicians, corporate heads, and many other personalities. This has changed the public relations area. Everybody needs to sell himself on this reality."

"It's important for people to understand this [need], overcome the fear of self-promotion, and not feel a self-revulsion about speaking up and letting others know what they do," comments Doe Lang. "In a hierarchy, the top people only know what is going on in detail if something slips up or isn't done. In order to make the positive part clear, people have to articulate that."

Doe Lang advises that the way to do this is "with pleasure and excitement. For example, a manager might say, 'I was so delighted that I was able to overcome the difficulties we had with shipping the product. My new plan will improve our ability to expedite orders in the future.' "

Lang suggests that "another way to become visible while being part of the information flow is to make events and achievements known by starting a bulletin board or newsletter for your department. The newsletter or bulletin board becomes a center of information itself. People come to you with what's going on, and this can give you real leverage in establishing allies, reaching out to people, and keeping aware of information that's important to know."

To sum up the subject of how to increase your visibility through personal public relations, most communication experts agree that when you project the attitude that it's a privilege to be part of a team that's bigger than any individual, you can promote yourself without turning others off. And when you genuinely feel that what you are doing is good for the company as well as for you, you can do it with a clear conscience.

CHAPTER 6

Making and Responding to Business Requests

"Will you please make time to work on this agenda today?"

"We've never done it that way before."

"I'm warning you—it won't work."

"You're always telling me what to do before you get the facts."

"You seldom give people credit for doing anything right."

"You don't want to listen to what I think."

"If you'd been clear when you gave that order we wouldn't have this problem."

As a manager, the chances are good that you've been confronted with reactions such as these from time to time when you've given orders or directions to others. But these responses and similar ones are negative and unproductive. They're also backlashes you can avoid if you use a good verbal approach when assigning work.

People's different behavioral makeups influence the way they respond when you make a business request. You need to tailor your method to each individual, although the following strategies have proved to cover most situations. By the way, these techniques also provide a verbal skill to show your promotion potential.

In this chapter we start with techniques for making work requests, then discuss how to respond to requests others make of you.

Giving Orders or Making Requests

There are four good ways to ensure that your orders will be carried out.

1. *Use a team approach.* Include your subordinates or peers in your request, with a "We're in this together" attitude rather than a dictatorial "Do this" approach.

"If you take time to tell people the purpose of a task, you get better results," points out Laura Hart, a New York City government press aid.

"Having them see the end product, so they know they're contributing to an overall mission, gives them the feeling they're team players rather than workers putting something together for which they don't see a purpose," says Dr. David Eyler, a former military manager and now manager of a private educational project.

Other managers are quick to agree that having a respectful, rather than condescending, relationship makes people more receptive and maximizes a manager's chances for seeing the orders executed. For example, instead of demanding, "I want

59

this now!" say in a pleasant tone, "Will you please make sure to work on this agenda today? As you can see, it's to go to John Doe regarding the conference that's scheduled for next month. He made a special request to see it as soon as possible. If you have any problem, see me and we'll work on it together."

2. *Be specific.* Explain what you want and when you want it. Let people know that what you say is what you mean, and then define the goals to be achieved and the standards to be met. Establish real rather than false deadlines; if you give too many false dates, the real ones won't be respected.

Good use of specifics when making requests includes:

"A board meeting is coming up the week of. . . ."

"The list of resolutions to be passed has to be presented next week."

"Someone from headquarters will be here to review the proposal on Monday."

3. *Offer praise.* You can elicit the behavior you want by praising that kind of behavior when it happens. For example, communications expert Doe Lang suggests, "If you say to people 'You never do that right' or 'You're doing a rotten job,' you can be sure they'll never do things right.

"On the other hand, if you make a point of noting any sign of behavior you've admired in the past—or any work procedure you've particularly liked—and then praise people for that behavior or procedure, they'll be able to amplify it." Lang emphasizes that this capacity to notice the positive things individuals do is a skill that greatly enhances other people's self-esteem and also improves their capacity to perform well.

4. *Monitor the progress.* Check periodically on how people are progressing with the jobs you have assigned. But don't burst into someone's office and ask combatively, "Where's that report?" or "Why haven't you done it?" Take a calmer approach, figuratively holding the person's hand and guiding him or her in a friendly way. Often just inquiring how people are getting along

and asking if they have any questions is a way of discovering what is—or isn't—being done.

Overcoming Objections to Your Requests

What can you do when you come face-to-face with objectors who drag you down with "It won't work" when you make requests? Often these persons have grievances behind their outward behavior. When you run into objections, try to determine the grievances your subordinates may have.

For example, Kathryn had been an assistant director in a large social service organization. When the existing director left suddenly, Kathryn was tapped for the job. This was a shock to most of her peers, many of whom thought they were as qualified as Kathryn and regarded the promotion as unfair. As their envy mounted, they banded together to sabotage Kathryn by objecting en masse to her orders and "forgetting" to carry them out.

It was a hard situation—and one that demanded diplomacy in the truest sense of the word. Kathryn knew she risked a "me" against "them" situation when she set up a meeting. But when she called the staff into her new office, she said in an easy, friendly way, "I care a great deal about your concerns and the way you regard this new situation, and I want you to know there's no reason in the world why we can't get along as usual. We've always been friends—and we're friends now."

But then Kathryn switched to a firmer tone and said openly and honestly, "Through circumstances beyond my control, I've been put in charge of managing the work that all of us must do, so I have to carry out policies and make requests of you. But my door will always be open to you, and I'll be committed to keeping on top of our mutual issues."

Laura Hart advises the person who meets objections to requests: "When managers offer that kind of commitment, it helps others feel a commitment as well. I've personally found that to overcome objections, managers must prove—or at least strongly imply—that there is a commitment on their part to keep on top of an issue and be there to respond to and participate in whatever comes up."

Here are four other approaches to use when employees object to your requests:

1. When giving a difficult order to which you expect objections, plan ahead and rehearse how you'll present it, then proceed slowly when you give the orders. Pay close attention to how your employee or employees react.
2. Take a deep breath and realize you don't have to respond immediately to every objection or view it as an attack on your position. As one experienced sales manager said, "I just sit there and nod my head. Then I go right on with what I meant to say. I figure I don't have to stop to take care of an objection which probably isn't the real objection anyway. I listen—but persist in my line of reasoning because I know when I'm ready to answer the objection it will still be waiting for me."
3. Ask employees to keep track of when what they're objecting to occurs—say, changes in their work procedures. When they get back to you with their objections, explain why you had to make those changes so that they will understand.
4. Show appreciation for their concern and use *please* and *thank-you*. This is a simple thing to do but too many managers forget their manners.

Coping With Closed-Minded People

All managers encounter situations when a negative higher-up refuses to listen to someone else's viewpoint. In one such instance, a department manager of a frozen foods corporation sold several people in the corporate hierarchy on the idea of setting up four seminars on pre-retirement planning. Since the suggestion was well received, the manager made a tentative arrangement with a retirement-planning consultant to present the four seminars.

All the details were in order except for the final seminar dates and contract signature. But before the contract could be signed the original comptroller was replaced by an individual whose single-minded purpose was fighting any unusual request for money. "With his patronizing, superior attitude, he tended to see the ideas of others as irrelevant," the manager declared, "so he had a closed mind about my request from the first day he came on the job. In fact, he was so against it he avoided talking to me."

Unfortunately, such closed-minded people are the sword of Damocles hanging over most managers' heads. If you don't meet them in one corporation, you're likely to see them in the next. There is no easy way to handle such people, but here are three approaches some managers have found effective:

1. Assemble your facts and backup material, and with a "There's something we need to talk about" approach, bring up the issue in a pleasant manner (no matter how hard that may be). Reveal your needs and discuss the company's needs, then ask the closed-minded individual for the adjustments you want. Even when you can't get your full request, you can sometimes improve the relationship to the point of a compromise solution.

"The dialogue you use to encourage compromise depends on the circumstance and situation," advises David Eyler. "But it boils down to seeking a common interest and trying to articulate the fact that you can establish a win-win situation if you work together and do things in a certain way."

2. Try to understand why your closed-minded peers act as they do and what image they have of themselves. Determine the qualities they value most, and let them know you recognize those qualities—again, in a way that isn't phony. Listen hard to what they say, then paraphrase their viewpoints and give their thoughts back to them. Because these persons like the idea that you listened and have understood what they said, they may be in a better frame of mind to compromise.

3. When the previous two tactics yield nothing, Dr. Eyler suggests the old political ploy of working around them. Use an

intermediary to communicate to the closed-minded individual that your ideas are valid and it's important to work with you.

Handling People Who Ignore or Dismiss What You Say

You're bound to be ignored or have some of your requests dismissed. Every organization has political involvements and situations in which groups have different interests that conflict with yours. "When that happens, a combination of political and communicative skills are called for," advises Dr. Eyler. "The main skill to use is making your point succinctly enough so top managers will grab hold of it."

In one such case, the manager in a federal agency presented a lengthy formal proposal for an innovative and timely program to a group of senior managers. But the senior managers were against the proposal ("We've never done that before") and immediately reacted with a committee-born response dismissing the entire idea.

But the manager switched tactics. He boiled down the proposal to a three-page presentation for the senior executives that detailed the dollar expenditure, issues, and personnel involvement. His verbal communication, before he presented his new proposal, was to "talk it out" with a wide range of people in various committees. He also spent time telephoning staff people on the senior executive team. Ultimately, the staff people latched on to the proposal.

Responding to Requests

Now that you've dealt with the problems of making requests, how do you handle the urge to complain when requests are made of you? Do you say yes, no, or maybe when responding to your boss's orders?

Newsletter publisher Don Bagin suggests, "Know how your boss likes to communicate. If he or she prefers choices that allow saying no to one idea and yes to another, provide choices."[1]

When You Want to Complain

When it comes to complaining, managers all want to do it sometimes, regardless of their management level. "We'd be martyrs if we didn't," admits Laura Hart. "But if you can make people aware of your current commitments and how much work you are already doing, it doesn't have to sound like complaining or lessen your credibility." Hart warns against seeming to attack or being on the offensive. Instead, she suggests that an honest and truthful response might be:

> "I think that maybe I shouldn't handle such and such a project this week because I'm already doing A, B, C, D, and E."

> "It's probably not very wise for me to try to handle this job, too, because I'm. . . ."

> "Frankly, I don't think I'm able to handle that additional task right now. There may be someone more appropriate to do it who is not doing as much at this time."

To keep from sounding like a complainer, choose your verbal approach carefully. As Dr. Eyler states, "It's how the words and thoughts are conveyed that makes the difference. When your precept is honesty and you're sufficiently busy trying to manage and juggle priorities, it's not hard to establish a link to a genuine priority and get people to understand that that's what has to have your attention at that time." He suggests another reaction for this situation could be, "I'd like to deal with this in the future and would be more than happy to talk to you about it then."

Some Other Situations

Quite apart from the major priorities—the long-term assignments that can be your shield—there are short-term tasks or immediate "to dos" that can easily lead to discord unless you use a good verbal approach. Here are three common situations.

1. *Your workload is too heavy.* When you're asked to do too many things, you need to ask to have your workload lightened, without injuring your image.

"Just as in responding in a noncomplaining way to the big requests that are made of you, the best way—again—is to be forthright and honest," says Laura Hart. She notes that sometimes you can use the same dialogue. For instance:

> "I'm a little overwhelmed, and I think that because I'm doing this range of things you might want to assign or reassign that task to someone else."

> "I'm not trying to throw the work off, but because I'm already working on A, B, C, D, and E, perhaps it will be in everyone's best interest if someone else takes on F because I won't be able to give it the fair and thorough attention that I should."

> "I'm not sure that I should take it on now. I'd like to make every effort to move on it, but perhaps it should be redelegated."

2. *Your boss gives you unreasonable deadlines.* Suppose on a Monday you're ordered to start preparing a series of detailed weekly financial reports your boss wants turned in every Thursday. There's no margin for error or emergencies with a time frame that's so tight. But an emergency does arise, and you miss your first Thursday deadline. Your boss storms into your office saying, "I gave you an order to do that report and get it out on time! If it's not on time for next week I don't know what I'll do."

According to Doe Lang, "When that happens you feel as though you've been run over, assaulted, or made to eat crow, and you have the option of collapsing meekly, fighting back, or saying nothing." But she notes that none of those responses is effective. "One good verbal response is to match the attacker's style, tone, and dynamics and turn the attack into a cooperative motion." For example, Lang suggests something like, "You're absolutely right in being angry. I am just as upset as you are that the copy machine broke down and that I wasn't able to assemble the material and do the report on time. In fact, I'm so mad about this that I'm going to be sure that next week's report is done a day ahead of time."

When you respond this way, says Lang, "the other person feels matched and is likely to simmer down with a 'Well, yes okay' change of heart."

3. *Your supervisor's instructions aren't clear.* A supervisor who gives no guidelines when assigning work invites problems later on. Doe Lang tells the story of an assistant administrator in a large medical complex who took over a job in a top administrator's office. In the first week it was obvious that the administrator excelled in giving ambiguous orders, whether for screening phone calls or drafting staff directives. He shot directions at her so fast she felt incompetent, even though she had functioned well in all of her previous jobs.

When asked how she was handling this, she answered "I freeze." Doe Lang suggested she first take a deep breath and realize that people with such behavior act that way to everyone. Then Lang helped her work out a communication strategy so the administrator would realize that, to get the kind of work he wanted, he would have to give certain input. The strategy was to go to him and say, "You know I think it will be important for you to give me really clear guidelines about what you would like me to do, how you would like me to do it, and when you would like me to do it. In that way I can do everything the way you like it done." Lang concludes, "Without being defensive and reproachful, that response went straight to the heart of the matter and put the administrator on notice that his behavior was unacceptable."

In the end, it's the spirit of cooperation that increases the chances that business requests will be carried out, whether you're on the giving or receiving side. And when you level about your side (while, at the same time, empathizing with the other side), the tools and techniques in this chapter will serve you well many times.

CHAPTER 7

Your Verbal Skills at Presentations and Meetings

"I have some worthwhile strategies I'd like to share with you."

According to a survey reported in *The Book of Lists*, people's single greatest fear is that of having to speak in front of a group. In fact, this fear by a two-to-one margin outranked the fear of death![1]

Nevertheless, stage fright is a fear no manager can afford to nurture. Surveys indicate that one of the skills most in demand for managers who want to progress up the corporate ladder is the ability to lead or take part in presentations and meetings.

One study, for instance—a Harrison Conference Services survey conducted at New York's Hofstra University—showed clearly that executives who know how to run productive business meetings are considered the most competent.

"Because most business today is conducted in groups, it's fair to conclude that if you can't manage a meeting, you usually can't manage,'' said Harrison Conference Services' chairman, Walter A. Green.[2]

Other managers are quick to point out that the opportunity to move ahead is built into most presentations because when higher authorities see a middle manager projecting a positive verbal image, they're more likely to view that person as a candidate for advancement. In fact, every manager interviewed for this book stressed that there are few situations where visibility is greater than in meetings and presentations.

Types of Meetings and Presentations

There are various types of business presentations for giving and gaining information, but all demand strong verbal skills. You can make the most of these chances to increase your visibility, varying your approach with the type of meeting.

Among the most common types of business meetings are:

1. Staff, board, upper-management, or committee meetings for presenting long- and short-range objectives and ideas, outlining plans of action, and seeking approval for projects
2. Meetings with stockholders, employees, consumers, vendors, government officials, and professional colleagues to report on the status of projects, plans, or programs, or to measure progress against objectives
3. Company-sponsored out-of-town seminars, workshops, and conferences
4. Public relations meetings for introducing new products
5. Sales and other motivational meetings for staff members
6. One-on-one meetings with a supervisor in order to present information or reports

There may also be occasions when you are asked to give a speech that relates to your area of expertise.

A Pre-Meeting Strategy

The most important initial strategy for an upcoming meeting is research and preparation so you (1) know your subject thoroughly, (2) are clear on what needs to be said and why it needs to be said, and (3) can establish a strong and credible point of view.

In training the members of its organization to prepare meetings, the California-based International Training In Communication (ITC) stresses in one of its leaflets:

> The speaker has great responsibility to prepare thoroughly so that his presentation projects the feeling "I have some worthwhile ideas and skills to share with you and in exchange I want your time and undivided attention which I promise will be well spent."
>
> If 35 individuals attend a two-hour workshop and it is useful, then seventy fruitful hours of individual learning have resulted from that workshop. Contrast that with seventy wasted hours for a poor presentation, and it is easy to recognize the heavy responsibility for preparation which rests with the speaker.[3]

To prepare adequately for a good verbal presentation, managers need to keep in mind the following pre-meeting strategies.

1. *Have a clearly defined objective for the meeting and each participant's role.* Is the purpose of the meeting to give out information? Gain information? Consider a current problem? Win acceptance of a plan? What information will each speaker present? Define your purpose as concisely as Toastmasters International, another California-based organization devoted to the improvement and development of communication skills, does in four examples of their objectives for an upcoming meeting:

> *Personnel manager*—to provide an overview of the company's history, organization, and products so that new employees can understand and relate to company goals and philosophy, and

see where they fit into the picture in terms of their contribution and responsibility.

Manufacturing plant division manager—to explain the support functions of another division on a particular project.

Managing industrial engineer—to brief line technicians in order to relieve their anxiety over possible production cutbacks.

Real estate broker or insurance sales manager—to brief his or her sales force on a particular economic trend that will influence future sales so that groundwork can be laid for a new marketing strategy or approach.[4]

2. *Know the persons you'll be talking to.* Determine whether they're in-house personnel or people outside of the home office. To prepare material so your audience will be receptive to your presentation, you must know where they're coming from and what issues really concern them.

"The more you know about why people are at the meeting and what interests bring them together, the more effective you can be," advises Dr. Donald L. Kirkpatrick, a management training and development consultant and author of *No-Nonsense Communication*. "As a preliminary to the meeting, you may want to tell them, 'There will be a meeting, and this is why we're calling it.' In that way you can attract interest and attention."

3. *Make up an outline of your presentation.* As you strive for new approaches and innovative ways to present your material, think through exactly what you want to say. Outline what you want to say on paper or index cards so you will have the essential facts in writing before you.

"The key word is to keep it simple," says Marcy Syms, president and chief operating officer of a chain of off-price clothing stores. "To be sure you do this, write down a few words that either lead into or sum up every point you plan to make. Later this will be your jumping off point for verbal discussion."

Highlight or underline the key words in your outline, and then arrange your material so that a few portions can be deleted if necessary. At the actual meeting, time-robbing events may occur beyond your control, and having parts of the presentation marked for elimination will help should you run short of time.

As you prepare your material, use a timer to check your time as you go along.

If using index cards, be sure to number them. This way you'll be spared embarrassment if you drop the cards and have to rearrange them. Also, when you use index cards it's a good idea to write the key ideas on a computer or word processor and paste them on the cards.[5] The clean, sharp print from a computer printout is usually easier to read than typewriter print or penmanship.

4. *Anticipate questions and reactions.* Don't let the audience's responses throw you off track or rattle you. Anticipate as many of these responses as you can.

Unless Lady Luck has a constant smile for you, chances are good that some meetings will have some adversaries. To prepare for this, have facts and figures ready, advises Mark Clemente, a marketing director. In fact, he advises anticipating every conceivable question. "List the toughest, most likely ones with which you might be hit, then formulate your verbal responses to them before you get to the meeting."

"Sometimes you're not the best judge of what the difficult questions will be, so if you're not working with a group, it can be a good idea to consult peers or superiors who are not involved in the meeting," says Marcy Syms.

In running your questions by them you can see what obstacles and negatives come to their minds. If you're working with a group to prepare a meeting, it can be part of the group's assignment that each person is responsible for determining—in his or her area—what the most difficult questions might be. I think if you prepare well there aren't too many questions that can throw you.

5. *Rehearse aloud before a mirror or with a tape recorder.* Consider a videotape rehearsal, too, since this is possible in more and more business settings. For your practice sessions, the International Training In Communication (ITC) Organization advises,

73

See yourself, actually visualize in your mind the verbal situation you are about to face. See yourself being introduced, walking with energy to the lectern acknowledging your introduction, opening your presentation. See yourself as poised and confident. See yourself concluding on a strong note. Dwell on these pictures in your mind. Program yourself for speaking success.[6]

The Event—Your Meeting or Presentation

When the time of your presentation arrives, your first step toward acceptance depends on the initial impression the attendees form of you. "Even when they already have an impression of you from the past, there will be a new first impression at each new meeting," says Marcy Syms. "That impression will be based on how well you've prepared, how sparkling your eyes are that day, how your voice sounds, how alert you are to your environment, and how succinctly you put forth what you plan to cover."

Here are some tips to make a favorable first impression.

1. *Approach the rostrum or head of the conference table in a positive and confident manner*. Pause before you speak, and take a few seconds to survey the situation and scan the attendees. You can be sure that while you do this, the attendees will be scanning you, too. Moreover, the moment you start to speak, they'll form a first impression of how you measure up in terms of energy, enthusiasm, information, knowledge, voice projection, eye contact, and gestures.

2. *Open the meeting on time*. "Too many managers don't begin on time," says Donald Kirkpatrick. "Instead, they resort to such statements as 'I guess we'll get started now.' " Rather than beginning in such a weak way, take a few seconds to smile and show your audience you're looking forward to presenting your material to them. If it's up to you to announce that questions and answers will follow your presentation, use your

opening-on-time moment to mention that questions should be held until then.

3. *Use an attention-getting opener.* You want the meeting to start on an upbeat note.

"As part of getting started, in cases when everyone does not know you and the other attendees, tell a little about yourself and your background," Donald Kirkpatrick advises. "You can also have people introduce themselves."

Sometimes, to warm the atmosphere and relax attendees, it's good to open with a light touch—some brief, appropriate and relevant humor that tempers the seriousness of your message. When you're speaking at a meeting away from home, for example, you could start with a comment on local happenings.

Donald Kirkpatrick describes two examples: "If I were giving a presentation in Green Bay, Wisconsin, I would say something about the Green Bay Packers. Or if I were running a luncheon meeting following the deer-hunting season, I'd start with an attention-getter about expecting a venison meal."

If the current meeting relates to a previous one, you could sum up briefly what was decided at the earlier meeting. But the main order of your business—and the *real* opener—is the point of your meeting. State concisely the topic or problem you've defined as the objective for the meeting. For instance,

"We're here to discuss our proposed price increases and the methods we'll use to tell our customers about it."

"The purpose of this meeting is to talk about our expansion program."

As soon as you define the purpose of your presentation, you should indicate you have a tight agenda. If you haven't previously handed out an agenda, with suggested ideas and plans, pass one out at this time.

"You may also want to go around the room and ask what the attendees' first reactions are," suggests Marcy Syms. "Sometimes those first reactions can bring up a direction you want to develop."

4. *Concentrate on problem-solving and suggested follow-up actions.* As you tell attendees what needs to be done, lead them through a logical approach to the solutions or to facts they can act upon.

- Explain the thoughts and ideas behind your proposed solution.
- Provide the necessary information they need to address the issue.
- Have all your facts substantiated by solid conclusive evidence.

Vary the pace of your presentation, speaking and pausing when you need to. A pause—without any "uhs" and "ahs"—can serve either to emphasize a point or to help you collect yourself if (even with the best preparation) you have lost a thought for a moment. Lace your logic with optimism, and show both the up and down aspects of the ideas or projects—but primarily emphasize the positive elements.

5. *Get other people involved.* In your pre-meeting strategy, you analyzed who the prospective attendees would be in order to make your material supportable. Now that you're standing in front of them, involve the group by asking for their ideas.

Speech specialist and consultant Sandy Linver has stressed in her book *Speak Easy* how effective speaking today means getting involved with the human beings who are out there. "The more detached you are, the less involved you are willing to get, the less you want to get to know your audience, the less successful you're going to be."[7]

With this in mind, make it clear you welcome feedback from others in resolving a problem or crisis. Ask people to share information and opinions. Toastmasters International suggests encouraging participation through the use of such phrases as "in our common experience," "considering our mutual concern," and "the value of our group effort."

"When you're willing to listen to other opinions on an idea, you sometimes get ideas you haven't thought of yourself,'' says Marcy Syms. She explains,

> At one time when we had the opportunity to take over additional space and double the size of one of our clothing stores, we had a meeting about it with the management of the store in question. We hadn't yet made a decision on what we wanted to do, so we asked for suggestions from others on how we might best use the space.
>
> Because we didn't give the impression that we had already made up our mind about expanding and had thought of everything on our own, we received some very good ideas that got us into the men's custom-suit business and provided a viable way of using the space.
>
> Moreover, the people who suggested the idea felt especially committed to it because it was one that came from them. It really worked out quite well.

Naturally, there will be some situations when people will offer opposing arguments, raise irrelevant points, or take advantage of their chance to talk and ramble on and on. When this happens, acknowledge the opposing arguments and then present evidence that supports your view. Dispose of irrelevant points with a comment such as, "Let's keep that for later. This is the issue right now."

When dealing with people who try to monopolize the meeting, follow the suggestions of *Communication Publications and Resources*. When long-winded people pause, direct the conversation to another person. For example, "Pat, I think this is a concern of yours, too. What do you think?" Or try a direct approach: "Les, we don't have a lot of time" or "We still have to deal with. . . ." When the long-winded speakers finally yield the floor, don't let them have it back again.[8]

6. *Be persuasive.* The ability to persuade other people is essential to good verbal communication. To be a winner at your meetings, you need to use all your verbal skills.

In her article "Friendly Persuasion," Linda D. Swink pinpoints the following tips for persuading people to feel or react as you do:

- Set a good mood and give them sufficient reason to sit and listen to you.
- Convince them that your needs and interests are similar to theirs.
- Help them see the magnitude of the problem or project.
- State your intentions and objectives so attendees do not feel they're being manipulated.
- Avoid distorting facts or suppressing key information.[9]

Swink cites the twelve most persuasive words in the English language, according to a Yale University study:

you	guarantee
money	love
save	discovery
new	results
easy	health
free	proven[10]

The Question Session

A question-and-answer session following a presentation has value because it both gives you feedback and provides an opportunity to reinforce your message or introduce new information. In addition, you can sometimes broaden the questions to expand on important phases of your main presentation.

When You Ask Questions

To obtain the input you want, frame your questions so they are open ended. "You don't ask questions that bring yes or no answers, and you don't state them in such a way that you give away what you expect the answer to be," explains Marcy Syms.

For example, I wouldn't say "Sales have been down for the last month. We know the consumer is not shopping as frequently as in the past. What do you think is wrong?"

When you phrase a question in that manner, you've already put people at the meeting in a certain frame of mind for looking at the answer. So rather than speaking that way, I might say at the meeting, "We're getting together to review our performance for the last three months. Does anyone see any trends?" In this way you can steer the meeting toward a discussion of why the trend is this way.

It's helpful to have participants at the meeting establish that for you, and it also lets your group members shine.

When you ask questions, encourage people to answer only the question you asked. If you don't keep a tight rein on their responses, there will always be attendees who use a question to say whatever is on their minds, whether relevant or not. This can be a great waste of time for you and the rest of the group. As Marcy Syms points out,

When people get way off the topic, you can say "That's an interesting point. Perhaps we can discuss it at another time, but I don't think with the information that we have to present now that that is part of this discussion."

On the other hand, if the other person comes back and says "Well, it is part of this discussion because of such-and-such" and then gives you solid reasons why it's relevant, you can't slough it off and seem to be avoiding something, without appearing to be giving a weak presentation.

One way to get around this is to use the old approach of answering a question with a question. For instance, you might respond with "I wonder if you could explain further what information you'd like to obtain from that question. What are you looking for?"

When You Take Questions

Keep the question-and-answer session moving by allowing several attendees to ask questions—one question at a time—and see to it that your answers are short and to the point.

Sometimes, when you first open for questions, attendees are reluctant to speak up. You can prime the pump by beginning with one or two questions of your own. For example, say, "One question that's always asked about this is. . . ." or "Right before I began my presentation I was asked if. . . ."

If you are asked a hostile question—one that's completely out of place—or if a question constitutes a personal or unfair attack on you, keep your temper under control and politely decline to respond.

When You Answer

The answers you give to legitimate questions should showcase your verbal skills. Toastmasters International advises that a good answer has the following ten characteristics:

1. It answers the question.
2. It is stated positively.
3. It is expressed in terms the audience can understand.
4. It is specific.
5. It is concise.
6. It puts the main point up front.
7. It does not include more information than is necessary.
8. It does not include loaded or slanted words used by the questioner as bait to set you up.
9. It capitalizes on opportunities in the questions to state or restate your point of view.
10. It doesn't sound antagonistic, evasive, or defensive.[11]

Regardless of how effectively you answer—and how thoroughly you anticipated the questions in your pre-meeting strategies—most question-and-answer sessions can turn into forums for confrontation with questions that are difficult to answer. Consider these three common situations and the ways to handle each one.

1. *When you don't know the answer.* Even though you are well prepared and knowledgeable about your subject, you will not know the answer to everything. That's all right. "Don't guess and don't hedge," says Doe Lang. "Offer to find out the information and send it on after the meeting or presentation."

New York Governor Mario Cuomo was on a television program one time when a woman in the audience asked a specific question about a certain bill. Cuomo responded with, "I don't know," explaining that hundreds of bills go through the legislature each year. With her name and address in hand, Cuomo said he'd find the answer and get back to her. If a governor can do this, a middle manager can, too!

2. *When you need a moment to think of an answer.* It's legitimate to take a minute or two to put your thoughts together. One technique is to rephrase the question, in the meantime giving yourself time to think. "You needn't feel that a momentary silence may be construed as a lack of interest or mental incompetence," Doe Lang points out. "You can always say 'Well, let me see. . . .' or 'That is something I've been thinking about.' "

3. *When a question doesn't require an answer.* Some people ask rhetorical questions. "If that kind of question is posed, ask yourself whether the person is really looking for an answer," advises Donald Kirkpatrick. "Then to respond to it, you can turn the question back to the person with 'How do you feel about it?' or 'You mean to say this is what you're thinking?' "

When You Wind Up the Meeting

Give some warning as you near the close of the question-and-answer session. Karen Berg, co-owner of CommCore Inc., a Manhattan communications consulting company, suggests you announce that you'll take one or two more questions. If the first of these questions is easy, or if you've made a positive statement in your answer, use that as an opportunity to exit. If you don't handle the question well, then take a second one to try to end on a positive note.[12]

Every Breath You Take

Despite your preparation and familiarity with your subject, there will be times when you feel nervous before a meeting or while talking to a group. This happens to most managers, but don't let stress take over. If your nerves get the upper hand, you'll find it impossible to speak at your best.

"When you're under stress you breathe rapidly and shallowly and don't get enough oxygen to your brain," explains Doe Lang, who produces tapes on breathing techniques and overcoming stage fright. "Most people breathe twelve to eighteen breaths a minute, so if you breathe more than eighteen you're under high stress. But if you can breathe slowly—seven breaths a minute or less—you can be perceived as authoritative and in command of yourself. Lang explains further,

> Naturally, breathing exercises have to be practiced, since most people breathe shallowly from the chest. But you have the opportunity to change the way you breathe every moment. [There are] wonderful examples of ad libs people have been able to come up with because correct breathing relaxed them and enabled them to have access to their intuition and say the right thing.

In one such case, Charlotte Ford, author of *Charlotte Ford's Book of Modern Manners,* was practicing Lang's breathing techniques before she was to talk to 1,500 people. As Ford listened to the chairperson introduce her, she made herself breathe slowly—even when she heard the chairperson say, "And now I want you to meet the son of Henry Ford." Because of her breathing and relaxation, Ford was able to stand up and respond graciously with, "Am I glad I wore my pants suit!"

Lang explains that, in another situation, an extremely attractive woman was introduced by a panel moderator with, "Are you married or single?" The question was inappropriate, but the woman had been practicing slow-breathing techniques and she quickly responded with "Independent." She evaded the question gracefully, and the audience applauded.

Visual Aids

Our focus in this book is on verbal communication, but a chapter on presentations wouldn't be complete without a reference to the visual aids that can so well illustrate your points and enhance your presentation.

In addition to such aids as handouts, which can outline the essential points you'll be covering, you may want to use one or more of the following in some way:

charts, graphs, and diagrams	physical models
posters	overhead transparencies
chalkboards	35-mm slides
flipcharts	films
magnetic boards	videotapes

Whichever visual aids you use, make sure each person, including those in the back, can see the material. When you use charts, graphs, posters, and boards, make the letters or numbers sufficiently large, with plenty of space between them.

Erase flipcharts or turn the pages before progressing to the next point. When you're finished with slides or films, turn off the projector so it won't detract from the rest of your presentation. And most important, practice in advance, using your visual aids, just as you rehearse your speech before going in front of the group.

The Conclusion of the Meeting

After your presentation and the question-and-answer session, lead people to take action by briefly and succinctly summarizing your objective and reinforcing your major points.

Following the summary, pick up your papers and notes and move away from the lectern—or wherever else you've been standing or sitting—with the same positive and confident manner as you showed when opening the meeting.

CHAPTER 8

Telephone Tactics

"Is this a good time to call you?"

How's your verbal IQ when you make or receive calls? Let's hope that your answer is good. As a manager, much of your communication is via the telephone, whether it's answering an inquiry, pitching a new idea, deciding a business matter, or (as so often happens) fielding a difficult call.

This aspect of verbal communication is also an essential skill for saving money and time. As Betty Lehan Harragan, author of *Games Mother Never Taught You,* has noted, "Skilled phoning is one way to reduce the flow of unnecessary material to your in box."[1]

But despite the importance of telephone communication, many managers fall short of being effective on the phone. "In fact, every day there are instances of people who handle themselves badly," points out Doe Lang, the communications expert. "Someone calls with 'Hi, how are you?' and you learn they want to send you something and have never talked to you before. Or another person says 'I'm Max' and you want to react with 'Who is Max—and why should I be talking to you?' "

Your Telephone Communication Skills

"Speaking over the phone is not really that different from talking with a person face-to-face," advises Susan Hayes, president of Results Design Group, an Ohio-based organization that specializes in total quality management consulting. "But when you're on the phone, people can't respond to you with visual reactions. *How* you say things is of prime importance, because often people respond to tone much more than they do to content."

While discussing tone and telephone communications in his book *No-Nonsense Communication,* Donald L. Kirkpatrick passes along these five tips from the Wisconsin Telephone Company:

1. Show alertness and interest by your tone. Give the person you're talking with your full attention.
2. Build a pleasant image with a "voice with a smile." Pleasantness is contagious.
3. Use simple, straightforward language. Avoid repetition of mechanical words or phrases—particularly avoid technical terms or slant.
4. Speak clearly and distinctly. Talk directly into the transmitter.
5. Use a normal range of tone for your voice and avoid extremes of loudness or softness. A well-modulated voice carries best over the telephone. Talk at a moderate rate, neither too fast nor too slow. Vary your tone of voice. It will add emphasis, help bring out the meaning of sentences, and add color and vitality to what you say.[2]

In addition, the following telephone tips are from *Briefings' Best Tips: Tactics and techniques to help you and your employees work smarter and succeed:*

1. Be sure all employees have the correct pronunciation of the names of your most important clients and customers.

2. Consider using telephone message slips that have a line for the phonetic spelling of a caller's name. This can help you avoid the embarrassment of mangling the name during the return call.
3. When using a speaker phone, always ask the person on the other end if you can be heard clearly. Many speaker phones sound hollow and some people don't like to deal with them.
4. Tape your voice at various times of the day when talking on the telephone. Then determine when your sound is at its best and its worst. Try to improve on the times when your voice doesn't seem as effective.[3]

When You Make Calls

Some of your calls will be business as usual, requiring common sense and telephone etiquette. Others will be crisis calls, which are never pleasant. Here are things to consider for both categories of calls.

1. *Collect your thoughts.* Have an idea of what you are going to say before you pick up the receiver. "I never pick up the phone cold," reveals Mark Clemente, marketing director for an accounting and management consulting firm. "Before I make a call, I've already scripted in my mind the introduction to my conversation or jotted down point-by-point what I want to say."
2. *Take notes.* Have a paper and pencil beside you and hold the phone with the opposite hand from the one with which you write, so you will be free for note-taking.
3. *Identify yourself immediately.* Explain at the outset who you are and what your business connection is. Start with a pleasant greeting such as, "How are you?" "How have you been?" or "How's everything?" Call people by name so they realize you know their name.
4. *Check if the time is right.* Remember that people may be

involved in something else when you call them, so indicate that you respect their time, and allow them a minute to shift gears. Use phrases that show concern and respect, and that prepare others for your verbal communication. For example:

"Do you have a moment to talk?"

"Do you have time to speak to me now?"

"Is this a good time to call you?"

"Do you have a minute to listen to some information I have?"

5. *Explain why you are calling*. State the purpose of your call immediately and quickly move into the business at hand. "The wisdom in business is that you have about thirty seconds to get someone's attention," explains David Eyler, program manager for a private educational project. Al Kelly, author of *How to Make Your Life Easier at Work*, agrees: "The most efficient managers rarely take longer than a minute on any phone discussion—about anything."[4]

6. *Allow time for reactions*. Even though your goal is to cover the business at hand quickly, give the person you call time to react to your comments. If you talk nonstop without a break, it can appear to others that you're reading from a script.

7. *Avoid side conversations*. Remember that while you're on the line, a side conversation or remarks to a third person in your office are thoughtless and out of place.

8. *Anticipate questions*. You may receive questions, so be ready to answer them. Mark Clemente cites his experience when calling someone from an out-of-town office about attending a meeting in the home office. The out-of-towner immediately reacted with, "Why should I make the trip?" A poor verbal answer would have been, "It would be good to have you here." Instead, Clemente had anticipated the question and answered, "You're an expert in your field, and some of the findings contained in the survey we'll be discussing fall into your area of

expertise. It would be valuable to have your input.'' In a turnabout, the out-of-towner responded, ''I would love to be there.''

9. *Keep excuses brief.* When returning a call that came in your absence, don't get hung up on such trivia as, ''I tried to get back to you earlier'' or ''I meant to call you yesterday'' or ''I attempted to reach you when I got your message but you were gone for the day.'' All that is past history and only delays attending to the present business.

10. *Don't put people on hold.* As much as possible, avoid putting people on hold when you're the person making the call. If the recipient has to look for information or obtain an answer to a question, you might be put on hold, however. ''If someone calls *me,* I definitely object to being put on hold,'' declares a quality control analyst. ''It aggravates me—and most managers I know—if my secretary says, 'Mr. Smith is on the phone' only to be told by *his* secretary, when I get on the phone, 'Please hold for Mr. Smith.' ''

Should You Place Your Own Calls?

Should managers place their own calls? There are divided opinions, and certainly there's no single answer. But many top-level executives like to have a direct line they can use themselves. In *Games Mother Never Taught You,* Betty Lehan Harragan reports:

> At top levels efficient executives install two lines; the first may be the company toy, the second ''private'' line is the instrument they use as a business tool, the one on which all important calls come and go, the one they answer themselves and dial (or push button) themselves. . . . The minor functionaries are the ones who set up elaborate screening systems; they think it makes them important.[5]

Donald Kirkpatrick advises, ''Place your own calls. You show interest and save time and money by placing your own calls. And, of course, make sure the line is not in use before you attempt to make the call. Place your own calls even if you have a secretary."[6]

"Make your own outgoing calls," stresses Al Kelly.

Don't ask your secretary to "Get me Mr. Rasputin please." Now you've got two people trying to get through—you and your secretary. Expecting the call will just create additional distraction from your other work. . . . Make it a habit to answer your own phone—even if you have a secretary or share one with others. It's a disgrace to the pin stripes to have secretaries answering calls all day with "Mr. Smurf's office," "Miss Cabbage's phone," and "May I ask who is calling?" What a waste of time! I find that at least five minutes per day of my own time is wasted by such delays with inside and outside calls. Imagine it—five minutes a day of every manager's time in every firm in the world wasted this way, plus the time of all those secretaries.[7]

When You Receive Calls

Just as you collect your thoughts before you make a call, when your phone rings get your head together as much as you can before picking up the receiver. Shift away from what you're doing so your mind will be clear to receive and handle the message or business coming to you. Obviously, you must do this quickly, because if you let your phone ring too long, your caller may hang up and you'll miss his message or business.

Here are some other recommended techniques for handling incoming calls.

1. *Take notes.* As when making calls, always have a pad and pencil beside you so you're ready to record the message. If you're not prepared to assimilate the information, you may have to ask callers to repeat themselves, thus giving the impression that you're not really listening.

2. *Give your name.* Identify yourself as soon as you answer, clearly stating your full name. Sometimes you may give
your department's name, too. In turn, start using your callers'
name as soon as he or she announces it.

3. *Get right to business.* Respond quickly without a lot of
"uhs" and "ahs." A good starter is, "What can I do for you?"
When you know the person calling you tends to ramble on, you
can always add, "You just caught me. I'm on my way to a
meeting and have to be there in five minutes." Many times that
will expedite business and cut out unnecessary details.

4. *Avoid transferring calls.* Handle the calls you receive
yourself and transfer them only if necessary. Donald Kirkpatrick advises that, if you must transfer a call, first explain why
you want to transfer it. For instance, say, "Mr. Brown handles
that. May I transfer you?" Kirkpatrick adds, "Be sure the
person who is calling wants to be transferred. If not, tell him or
her that someone will call back. For example, say, 'I will be
happy to have someone call you with this information.' "[8]

5. *Avoid long pauses.* If you must leave to check something, return promptly. "It's courteous to ask "Will you wait,
or shall I call you back?" points out Kirkpatrick.

If your caller waits use your hold button if your telephone has
one. If your telephone does not have a hold button, lay the
receiver down gently. If it takes longer than you expect to obtain
the information return to the line every half minute or so with a
progress report. You might say "Mr. Jones, I'm still checking on
that for you." When you return to the line be sure to get the
caller's attention. For example, say "Thank you for waiting."[9]

6. *Use hold button when necessary.* As the recipient of a
call, it's permissible to put people on hold politely when you
must leave the line to obtain information. Al Kelly also points
out that if another call comes in while you are speaking, you can
rightfully say, "Hold on a moment, please." According to Kelly,

Take the other line and say "I'm on another call. Can you hold?"
Usually this caller has only a trifling bit of news and will say

something like "No, I just want to say pork bellies went up six cents yesterday." You say "Okay, thanks, that's good." Then you revert to the first caller who now realizes that another interruption could occur and will expedite the rest of the discussion.[10]

Some Special Situations

There are certain unexpected telephone encounters, such as being confronted by an angry colleague or not understanding what a caller is saying, that challenge the best telephone skills. Here are some tactics for handling these difficult situations:

Stalling for Time

No matter how much you collect yourself before you answer the phone, there will be times when you pick up the receiver and find, for one reason or another, that you need a bit more time before you can speak up effectively with a well-handled response.

There are several stopgap phrases that will buy you time. Note, however, that you don't want to overuse these, since most people are aware of them and know they are a means of gaining time.

"My other phone is ringing. I'll get right back to you."

"I have someone on the other line. May I call you back?"

"There's someone in my office right now. I'll cut the meeting short and get back to you."

"Do you mind waiting while I check that for you?"

Of course, at the end of the waiting period you need to thank the person for waiting.

"It's my opinion that when you need to play for time to get an answer, you should say so rather than 'My other phone is ringing' or 'May I call you back,' " suggests Dr. Paula Kurman, director of Communicational Judo.

Sometimes I would rather say "You caught me short" and "I'm in the middle of a whole bunch of other things, and I'd rather not give this short shrift."

I personally advocate directness and think there needs to be an appreciation of the importance of the matter and a direct request for time. You can say to the person on the other end of the line "I can see this is an important issue, and I'm not sure exactly how I want to respond on this." Instead of giving you a quick answer, which in a sense demeans the importance of what you're saying, I'd rather take fifteen minutes, a day, or whatever time it needs and call you back after giving it serious and thoughtful consideration.

There are other verbal responses that help you field a difficult call. They give you a chance to collect information while also showing that you're considering the caller's need.

"I want to give this my full attention, so I'll check into it and get back to you."

"I have some ideas on that. Can I get back to you on them?"

"I'm unable to talk to you now. But I know this situation is important to you. Will you be available at 10:00 A.M. Wednesday? I'd like to talk to you then."

"I don't have that information now, but I'll be happy to locate it and call you back tomorrow."

"I'll be glad to take care of that for you. Can we schedule another call on this for Friday?"

Getting Caught Short

Suppose you receive a call and you don't know what the caller is talking about. We've all been caught short at one time or another. People phone and either use terms and expressions we don't understand or ask us to answer questions or assume responsibility for something we feel we should know more about. Perhaps you had no idea what the caller was speaking of, yet felt that if you admitted your ignorance, you might lose out on something.

There are varying strategies you can use to save your corporate face. One approach for handling this situation is to say something ambiguous, such as:

> "Can you define what you mean by? . . . I'm not quite sure of everything you mean by the way you're using that term."

> "I'm not completely clear about every aspect to which you may be referring, but I'll obtain full information for you and get back to you."

> "I'll research an in-depth answer for you and call you back to. . . ."

Another approach is to let the caller assume you understand what he or she is talking about, and then as soon as you hang up, you call someone else who can explain what it's all about. For instance, in one difficult situation a new vice-president of an international marketing firm was asked by the business editor of a widely circulated suburban newspaper to write a bylined article on his company's software package and on its plans for new software and hardware products.

This article was a chance for the new vice-president to showcase both his company and himself. Moreover, he felt the article would bring him speaking engagements and, in turn, his speeches would promote him as an expert in the computer field. He was already envisioning his byline on the page when the editor, an old-time newspaper man, said, "Be sure you give us just four takes. That's all we'll be able to handle."

At that point, the vice-president had no idea what the editor was talking about. He ruefully admitted, "I couldn't bring myself to call back and admit my ignorance. My solution was to get right back on the phone and call another paper to ask, without giving my name, what the term *takes* meant." When he learned that before the era of video display, newspaper people used *takes* as a term for pages (which copy boys would *take* to the composing room), he wrote and polished four pages and got them into print.

Appeasing an Angry Caller

You missed a delivery deadline and a customer is angry. How do you handle the call without getting angry yourself?

For example, the manager of the boys' sporting goods department in a large manufacturing firm sat red-faced at his end of the line while an angry customer yelled into the phone. "What kind of an outfit are you? You promised those nylon baseball jackets in time for our $11.95 sale, and we've already advertised them in this week's sale circular. Now some jerk from your place says the jackets aren't available. What kind of a screw-up is this, and what do you expect me to do?"

"The customer went on and on," the department manager said, "and his tone was getting me angry too, as the sweat poured out. But I couldn't let my anger show, so I calmly said to him, 'Can I ask you to hold a second while I see what we can do?' Then I moved the receiver away from my ear, took a deep breath, and said to myself, 'Okay, what do I say?'

From our point of view, a production problem had affected the availability of the jackets. But from the customer's viewpoint, we were in the wrong, so all I could do at this time was apologize and pacify him the best way I could.

Consequently, I got back on the phone with a "Sorry I had to put you on hold" and an apology for the inconvenience. Then I told the customer we'd substitute another type of boys' spring jacket that would normally sell at a higher price for a price that would meet the $11.95 he'd advertised for his sale. I also promised to see personally that he got an immediate shipment.

Suppose, in this same situation, the department manager had been unable to offer instant action during the telephone call. He should have gotten back on the line (once he'd caught his breath) and told the customer calmly, "I certainly understand how you feel, and you have every right to react this way, too. I'll look into this problem immediately and make it my top priority to see that you get a comparable product at the agreed-upon price in time for your advertised sale.

"I can't tell you what the substitution will be while we're on the phone today, but I'll check into what's available and get back to you tomorrow. We'll work out this crisis to your satisfaction, and in the future we'll make every effort to avoid a repeat of this problem."

There's a good chance the hostile customer would have calmed down at these words and agreed to sit tight until the following day to see what the manufacturer could offer in the way of a substitution. And this is just one example of how this type of verbal approach will buy a manager extra time when coping with an angry phone caller.

Giving Bad News

When faced with having to pass out upsetting information, most managers feel the telephone is an inadequate vehicle for giving full weight to the negative news. Nevertheless, sometimes it is the only means of communication and therefore they choose their words carefully. As the sales manager of a women's specialty chain says,

I temper these crisis, hard-to-handle calls by saying to the salespeople under me, "Look, Bud [or Mary or whomever],

I'm not calling you to upset you, but I do want to let you know that we have some problems to deal with that aren't all hunky-dory. I'm outlining them in a letter you'll be getting in a couple of days.''

While I don't give them the full hit of the bad news on the phone, I find a phone call effectively prepares them for the letter that's coming. And since most people want to put off bad news as long as possible, most of the salespersons I call don't pound on me for ramifications of whatever the details may be.

If they say, "Give me one little hint about what's up," I may give one little hint. But usually when they do push me I simply say, "No, I think it's better for you to read through the letter. Then you can digest the information and see how you feel about it. After that we'll be able to talk and come up with a plan of action." Generally—and literally—this approach gets me off the hook.

Saying Goodbye

The wheels of management only keep moving if you can conclude a business call as efficiently as possible. Close the call and hang up. Generally, telephone etiquette decrees that the person who makes the call concludes and hangs up first; most of the time, it's advisable to wait for that to happen. But as we all know, some people never make a move to do that. When stuck at an impasse, some managers pretend to be cut off, simply by hanging up on themselves while talking. The reasoning behind this is that a talkative person on the other end would never expect you to do this to yourself—unless the person is aware of this trick.

I recommend that you *not* close in this manner. Instead, try to say goodbye in a friendly manner that will leave the caller feeling satisfied. Along with, "Thank-you for calling" (and depending on the situation), here are three examples of good closings:

"I'll call you next Monday with my answer."

"I'll get back to you if I have any questions."

"Thanks for the information."

In the final analysis, no matter what kind of call you're handling, your interested and respectful attitude can combine with a clear, straightforward approach to add up to a high telephone verbal IQ that presents you at your corporate best. In essence, talking on the telephone is not much different from talking with people face to face.

CHAPTER 9

A Better Approach to Training

"I want you to succeed, and I'll do all I can to help you."

According to Andrew Sherwood, chairman and chief executive officer of the Goodrich and Sherwood Co., a human resources management consulting firm, the willingness to train and develop other workers is a prime managerial skill that companies and corporations desire.[1]

When managers excel in this skill, word gets around and it strengthens their visibility and upper-management potential. "But very few managers have been trained sufficiently on how to train and develop subordinates in in-house training programs," notes Dr. Donald L. Kirkpatrick, who is called in by major companies in the United States and abroad to evaluate training programs and work with managers and supervisors on the tools and techniques of effective training.

"Empathy" is a very popular word in the training and development field. Most teachers, it seems, use the word just like they use "motivation" or "leadership" or "communication." Although there are a variety of definitions, there is general agreement that a practical definition is "putting yourself in the other person's shoes." An old Indian proverb states, "Don't criticize a person until you have walked in his moccasins." Someone said, "You can't tell what persons are thinking by looking in their eyes; you must get behind them and look through their eyes to know what they are thinking or feeling." These are examples of "empathy."[2]

Other training consultants agree that expertise and empathy, based on proven verbal approaches and behavioral principles, enhance a manager's reputation. "But you *must* use a verbal approach that will bring people into the training process as participants rather than merely receivers," states Don Christman, a training consultant specializing in the banking and financial service industry. "If you aren't articulate, you won't last long as a trainer."

To sample viewpoints and gather suggestions on how managers can develop good verbal communication skills, I interviewed consultants who, on a day-to-day basis, teach managers how to train their personnel. Since they all emphasized that good training requires good verbal skills, this chapter explores their suggestions for how you can implement effective training programs and make your expertise more visible.

The Word Gets Around

"Any time you conduct a training program, word of mouth goes out on how you handle it," comments Don Christman, "and the word that is passed around will be, 'This is good and something you ought to take' or 'Don't waste your time on that.'"

Christman and other trainers point out that one way to automatically gain a good reputation as a training person is to motivate your trainees by bringing all of them into the process and acknowledging their contributions. They also stress that to be a successful trainer you need not only good subject matter but also top-notch verbal techniques for presenting the program, since *how* you train has as much to do with the success of a program as the subject matter itself.

Nine Ways to Motivate Trainees

There are several ways you can make your training more effective—and thus also gain a good reputation as a trainer.

1. *Define your training goals clearly.* At the start of a session, give a succinct ten-minute introduction that spells out (1) the purpose and content of the program, (2) the goals to be achieved, (3) the standards to be met, and (4) the fact that the program is a joint project—you are in this together and you are on the trainees' side. In this way, the people you're about to train know what to expect from you and what you expect from them.

"If I were about to train someone, my attitude would be 'Look, Mary, I want you to succeed, and I'll do all I can to help you,' " says Milo Sobel, a former manager of training and development for Citibank in Manhattan and now a management educator who trains managers at various learning centers and major service-oriented organizations.

I'd point out that I expected nothing less than that person's best efforts in return and add "But with your and my efforts combined, I'm confident you'll do a terrific job."

That approach is both firm and supportive because at the same time as you let people know that you'll knock yourself out for them, you make it clear that they have to do the work and are not getting off the hook thinking you're going to do it for them.

As a personal goal, managers need to instill a sense of fairness in themselves and avoid showing favoritism if they're training more than one person. That sounds obvious, but it isn't. So ask yourself as you train, "Have I been fair to so-and-so?" or "Have I spent as much time with John as I have with Mary?"

2. *Establish and maintain their interest.* "A key to getting people's attention and interest is to let them speak up and address their agenda first, and then tie yours into that," comments Milo Sobel. "When you do that you immediately establish their interest level and achieve a good natural flow of verbal exchange."

"Another way of getting people involved is by asking questions—and even asking for war stories," adds Don Christman. "But maintain a sense of discipline when you do this so you continue to hold the reins."

In their *Briefings' Best Tips,* the editors of *communication briefings* recommend acting more like a coach than a commander, and urge motivating people by being employee centered rather than productivity centered.

When you give oral explanations or directions, focus the listener's attention on what you're saying. Here's how: Lower your voice to force the listener to concentrate harder on your words. Shift your position as if to move closer to draw attention to you and what you're saying. But don't actually move. That would divert attention from what you're saying to what you're doing. Use a pad and pencil. Emphasize your key points with lines, arrows, stars, or dots. Sketch to help the listener visualize operations or procedures. Rough diagrams are effective when they're accompanied by verbal explanations."[3]

3. *Bring people back if their attention wanders.* If you see a person drifting away with a distant look in his or her eyes use the old trick of calling on that person. Depending upon the situation and subject matter say:

"How would you apply these precepts in a sales call, Bruce?"

"What kind of reaction would you expect from your staff after using the approach we've just discussed, Jane?"

"From a personal point of view, how will the techniques we've outlined help you, Bill?"

These and similar questions will almost always bring people back because we all hate to be caught asleep by a trainer and our peers.

4. *Ask why people challenge your assertions and techniques.* When you are challenged for one of your assertions or facts, Milo Sobel suggests exploring why the person objects to what you say and what he or she would have liked you to say. He adds,

But be prepared for these encounters, and whenever possible go into your sessions with solid references to back up your assertions. Then if someone says, "Where did you hear that nonsense?" and you can answer, "I just heard it from the chief executive" or "It's in our annual report on page 69," you'll hold the winning hand as objectors shrink under the table.

Don Christman explains a tool he uses when someone mistakenly challenges the validity of an assertion or technique. "I turn the technique I'm advocating back on the person as a means of clarifying how it works." He explains,

Let's assume, as a trainer, you're conducting a program in which you lay down certain precepts at the beginning—say a sales training program in which you're dealing with verbal skills. If someone takes exception to one of your techniques right up front, turn to that person and say:

"Exactly why do you feel that way?"

"Can you help me out a bit by elaborating on that further?"

"If I understand you correctly you said thus-and-so. Is
that right?"

By turning things back to the person in this manner, you
can get that individual to put on record—verbally—where
he or she is coming from. Since you know your techniques
are valid, you can take it from there and use the verbal
techniques you're suggesting to show they *really* work.

Generally a couple of people in the group will note that
you're using the techniques that were challenged on the
person who questioned them. Then, as the group sees [the
techniques] working, someone speaks up and says "See, he
just used that technique on you."

You get the group on your side in that way, and by
letting the other person off the hook through saying, "You
see how it can work," you usually obtain that person's
agreement too, and get him on board and into the training
process.

5. *Face up to a wrong precept or assertion.* If a true fact
refutes your original position, acknowledge that and change your
position.

For instance, even though most objections to your techniques can be handled as Don Christman has suggested (or
sometimes simply by ignoring them if the source is a lightweight
one), Christman explains that a serious objection posed by
someone with status in the organization needs to be dealt with
differently.

In certain situations, despite top-notch preparation, sometimes information wasn't available earlier. If it later turns out
that facts are against you, face the reality that you may have
been wrong.

"It's healthy to admit that," reports Christman:

Because you will be seen as a person (a) who is interested
in getting at the true situation, (b) who is verbally adept at
creating the kind of dialogue that enables that to happen,

104

and (c) who is big enough to admit your own position is wrong, based on your original, insufficient understanding of the situation.

A lot of people try to hide behind excuses and get up on positions they won't climb down from, so persons who don't do this are noticed in organizations and looked at as managers with upward potential.

The reverse is also true. You can use the techniques I've cited to push your own case home and, if your case is the stronger one, create a situation where you can isolate the other's position, demonstrate your strength, and move forward.

6. *Monitor your trainees' progress and give them feedback right from the start.* "Monitoring and feedback can take several forms," declares Milo Sobel:

For example, you can call participants or subordinates and say, "Just thought I'd touch base with you. I know you were doing well yesterday. But I thought you might have some questions or comments that will help you get more out of the training. Anything else we can discuss?"

If the subordinate says, "No, I'm doing fine," you can answer, "Great! I'll look forward to seeing you tomorrow."

But some people—instead of saying "I'm doing fine"— may come up with questions they're embarrassed to bring up in a training session because they mistakenly think that everybody else knows the answers. Since they believe they're the only ones who don't understand everything they feel like idiots.

When you're the manager who is training employees on the job the following tips from trainers will also help you motivate people.

First, if you're concerned about a personality trait—perhaps a trainee never speaks up—mention that concern to the person's boss (if you're not the in-house boss yourself). When you use good judgment here and remember to also stress positive traits, the boss can later say to the person, "I was talking to your trainer, who thinks you have a great deal to offer and wishes you'd contribute more in class." That positive feedback may encourage a person to participate.

Similarly, if someone is doing especially well, pass along that word. Then a boss can tell the person, "I got a call from your trainer, and she said you've really made a great contribution. Congratulations, and keep it up."

Last, supplement verbal pats on the back with morale-boosting memos.

"Little things like that have a lot of value," Sobel points out. "You can write 'Dear John, enjoy having you in the course. Keep up the good work.' Then you can either carbon copy that memo to the person's boss or send a direct memo—such as 'Dear Bill, just wanted to let you know it's a pleasure to have John in my course. He has contributed a great deal.' John will get that feedback from the boss and come back with even more motivation to do well."

When you take time to do this follow-up motivation it's in the trainee's, the boss's, and your best interests. The trainee and his or her boss will appreciate your help and concern, and you, as a manager, will be regarded as a trainer with empathy and expertise.

7. *Show ongoing support.* You can build a good reputation as a trainer by monitoring your trainees and giving them feedback right from the start. Likewise, your continued support and help will also spread the word on how well you train your employees. "When you try to bring out the best in others, you bring out the best in yourself," stresses Milo Sobel.

Occasionally, managers question whether motivating others with an eye to enhancing their own reputation is self-serving and a form of manipulation. "That's a legitimate concern," acknowledges Christman, "because no one wants to appear to be a puppeteer pulling other people's strings—and that's good. On the other hand, any process in which you engage in dialogue with other people and try to persuade them to your point of

106

view is inherently manipulative because you're trying to create verbal mechanisms that will achieve this.''

Paula Kurman, the director of Communicational Judo, Inc., affirms this: ''There's nothing really wrong with the kind of manipulation that is honest, open, and up front. It isn't bad when the other person is considered, too. It's the pretending that's bad.''

Rather than viewing it as self-serving manipulation, most trainers feel that an empathetic approach highlights the mutuality of interests. It relates to a company's planned goals, making it advantageous to both manager and trainees. Don Christman offers an example:

> If a company's strategic plan or goal calls for emphasizing six banking services because they've been found to be among the most profitable, any excellent level of achievement in marketing those services by the bank's staff helps the bank to implement its plans for profitability. A manager can build and enhance motivation by pointing out how helping achieve that goal will work to everyone's advantage.

Likewise, Milo Sobel emphasizes that ''those mutualities of interests are the keystones of what managers are involved with in training others.'' He adds,

> In fact, the underlying message that continues to motivate people might well be a paraphrase of the Vidal Sassoon television commercial, ''If you don't look good, we don't look good.'' That paraphrase—worded positively—could say in management, ''When you look good, I look good.'' Conversely, ''When I look good, you look good'' makes subordinates try to make you look good. That's really the key to it.

8. *Accentuate the positive.* ''Always frame what you say in positive rather than negative terms,'' stresses Don Christman. ''For instance, when providing feedback on a task, avoid such

rights or wrongs as, 'You shouldn't have done that' or 'That was bad.'

"Instead, the preferred approach is 'Do you think it might have been more effective if you had done thus and so?' and 'How do you feel about that?' This solicits opinions and facilitates discussions."

Milo Sobel also emphasizes the need to be positive. In one situation, a middle manager consistently left the conference room as a paper-strewn mess after each training session. Naturally, the next group to use the room complained about the shambles. The ineffective approach to the problem would have been to tell the manager he was a slob. But as Sobel explains, a positive verbal approach worked well:

> The effective way to resolve it was to say, "I've always admired your creativity and the way you can jot so many things down in such rapid order. I know it's part of the creative process to jot things down and then throw out the notes you don't like—and I don't want to hamper your creative process. But, please, if you wouldn't mind, will you get all those scraps off the table and the floor before the next group comes in?"

9. *Motivate by example*. Sometimes setting an example is difficult in today's corporate environment, where rules and hierarchies are set in place. But some effective managers can motivate by example regardless of their rank. For example, when Sonny (David) Werblin was president and chief executive officer of the Madison Square Garden Corporation, it was common to see him in the halls of the arena, stooping down to throw away discarded hot-dog rolls. This is motivation by example at its very best! Certainly it's a safe bet that the persons responsible for the trash worked double time the next day.

Toward a More Positive Vocabulary

The preceding pages offer some smart verbal approaches for training employees. Here are some others you can incorporate into your training vocabulary.

"How can I help you?"

"Do you think that? . . ."

"Would it be a good idea to consider? . . ."

"What alternatives would you suggest?

"Are you comfortable doing it this way rather than that way?"

"What would you have liked me to add that I didn't say?"

"What was it you didn't like about what I said?"

"I'm always accessible."

"I want you to feel I'm on your side."

"Do you see how this procedure can work?"

"Do you agree?"

In selecting phrases to use, pick key words and questions that solicit yes responses. Don Christman advises,

If at the end of a session the participants' comprehension of your training remains implicit rather than explicit, the understanding you've worked toward tends to get fuzzy after the dialogue ceases.

But if you're on record with such answers as, "Yes, I agree" or "Yes, I think *A* is better than *B*," your training remains with people longer. They have verbally assented to certain propositions which affect how they conduct themselves afterwards.

As a final suggestion for training with expertise and empathy, Milo Sobel recommends letting employees know their managers are always within reach for support and help.

"Whether it's a formal training course or training someone for a specific job, it's my personal style to say, 'As far as I'm concerned this training never ends. Because we can always learn I'm always accessible, and I want you to feel that I'm on your side forever.' People like that," he concludes. "It makes them work even harder for you."

CHAPTER 10

Giving Effective Performance Appraisals

"It's critical that we agree on objectives."

In his book *Let's Talk Quality*, management consultant and educator Philip B. Crosby writes that the basic idea of a performance appraisal is to give employees real input into the system, including evaluating the management.

Performance appraisal is one of the most important things managers can do, but hardly anyone does it well. It always bugged me that someone I didn't choose got to make decisions about my career.

Only one person I ever worked for in my early years thought I was capable of more responsibility. I usually received the "we-don't-think-you-really-are-the-person-for-the-job-but-we-don't-have-anyone-else" routine.[1]

Crosby reports that the only good performance review he ever had was put together by his boss at a company where he was a manager earlier in his career. What that particular boss did was to assemble the six or so other managers with whom Crosby dealt regularly. Then the boss held a no-holds-barred discussion about Crosby and his performance. Following that meeting the boss summarized the results and discussed his report with Crosby.

"What I learned was how I appeared to people, some changes I needed to make in my relating and managing style, and some places where my communication skills were inadequate," reveals Crosby. "It was a great thing and I carried a copy around with me for years."[2]

Since many managers at all levels lack the expertise for giving performance appraisals, another way to stand out in a corporation is to develop good verbal skills for evaluating your employees' performance and for encouraging them to improve their performance.

"If you do it automatically, just to meet the requirements of your organization—that is, you talk with each employee once a year, check the items on a form, have the employee sign it and send it in—you are not doing your job effectively," advises Natasha Josefowitz, author of *Paths to Power* and a consultant to industry, government, and service organizations. "Its purpose is not to comply with company regulations once a year; it should be used as an incentive to keep the communication active throughout the year."[3] This chapter discusses how to develop those verbal skills to make performance appraisal your management strength.

The First Step

An effective performance review should provide your employees with (1) an understanding of what you expect from them, (2) your view of their strengths and weaknesses, and (3) your evaluation of how well they're meeting the standards and objectives of both the job to be done and their future careers.

To give an effective performance review—and also to coach your employees throughout the year—your first step should be to spend some time by yourself. You need to think through what the employee has done, as well as determine what about that person's performance needs to be improved.

Natasha Josefowitz suggests that you also ask the following questions:

1. What are my objectives for this interview?
2. What do I need to talk about with this person that might be helpful?
3. How would I like this person to feel when he or she walks out of here?
4. How do I accomplish that?[4]

It's also important to ask yourself whether you like or dislike the person you're about to review. Remind yourself that a performance evaluation is only about *job performance*—it's not an evaluation of a person. Because we're human, it's vital to check for personal bias and to avoid reacting to people because of who they are or because they may remind us of someone we don't like. As Josefowitz points out,

> I know my own danger signals. If I am anxious about doing a performance evaluation, if I feel some fairly strong emotion, then a little flag is raised inside of me that says "What are you reacting to?" I pay attention to this and really try to think through what is going on inside of me. It's very important to not be controlled by my emotions so that my responses to that person are fair.
>
> The other danger signal I recognize in myself is when I think about the person in terms of what she or he *is* as opposed to what she or he *does* on the job.[5]

The Appraisal Itself

Many companies have formal procedures or forms to be used for evaluating an employee's performance. But whether or not your company has specific guidelines, Natasha Josefowitz suggests you start your review by asking employees a few probing questions that will let you know their perception of where they stand. It is hoped that they've evaluated themselves prior to the meeting with you, so they'll have answers ready to such questions as:

1. What do you think of your performance?
2. Are you generally satisfied or dissatisfied with your productivity?
3. What do you think of the job in terms of variety, challenge, and security?
4. How do you get along with your co-workers? Where do you hope to go in this job?
5. What are your career objectives?[6]

After you listen to their responses, according to Josefowitz, it's your time to speak up. Give your perception of their past and present performance, and explain how you feel about their work. You can begin by (1) identifying and reinforcing the components of the job and (2) defining the goals and objectives to be achieved and the standards to be met.

As you do this, be honest about the behavior and performance you want. Clarify specifically what you expect of them. Talk about how successfully—or unsuccessfully—the job objectives have been met. And be able to confirm your observations with written data.

While going over objectives, discuss with your employees the traits that need improvement. Delve into how well your objectives and your employees' objectives complement each other. Since it's critical that you agree upon objectives, determine the following:

- Which of their objectives can you agree with?
- Which of your objectives can they agree with?
- When can you both expect to have your objectives completed?

114

During the appraisal, do your best to help your employees improve by asking questions such as, "In what way can I be more helpful?" or "What can I do to help?" Ask if progress reports throughout the year would be beneficial. Could they do their jobs more effectively if large projects were divided into smaller, easier-to-handle segments, for instance?

"Give them as much responsibility as you can in figuring out their own solutions," states Natasha Josefowitz. "You may need to help with suggestions, but your job is to pose the questions and then be available to evaluate their solutions."[7]

Three Keys to Better Appraisals

To enhance your reputation as a manager who's effective in evaluating employees' performances, make it your business to:

1. *Be generous with your praise and recognition of good jobs.* Although being specific and honest in your evaluation necessitates giving negative feedback at times, try to stress positive elements as much as you can. Use such phrases as, "You deserve a medal for. . . ." and "That was great work."

In speaking of a manager's tendency to give negative rather than positive feedback, the communications expert Doe Lang tells the story of the child who didn't speak until he was 6½ years old:

> One day at breakfast he said to his mother, "This cereal is cold." The shocked mother immediately responded, "Oh, my goodness, you can speak. Why didn't you say anything before?" To that the child answered soberly, "Everything was okay up till now."

"Admittedly, that's a highly unlikely story," declares Lang, "but it's a marvelous illustration of the way we're not

115

trained to give positive feedback. Instead we're more trained to give negative feedback.''

2. *Give top attention to key people who perform well.* According to *Briefings' Best Tips,* "Too often we spend extra time with employees who need help and who aren't producing as well as we would like. The producers are the ones who will make the major difference for you. Encourage them."[8]

3. *Be prepared to handle objections and excuses.* When an objection or excuse is raised, Tony Cipollone, training director of the Kentucky-based Metroweb Corporation, advises turning the objection back to the person and asking him or her to explain further what he or she is talking about. "If the objection is, in fact, an excuse or if the person seems to be dismissing what you say, then that person needs to be challenged."

Depending on the situation, Cipollone suggests that you might say:

"You seem to be dismissing this very simply."

"What is it that's behind your objection?"

"Why do you as an individual seem to be opposed to this?"

"I'd like a little better explanation or further discussion on why you think this isn't going to work."

"I don't understand how your objection holds water."

"Many people will give you a 'here's-what-I'm-thinking' kind of answer, which is satisfactory up to a point," explains Cipollone. "But then if the objection still doesn't make any sense or if I feel that I've refuted it and that it's simply invalid, I go to the *feeling* rather than the *thinking* level and say, 'I don't agree that this is anything that's standing in the way. There's something else and I wonder if you could try to get to that.' "

Once objections and excuses are resolved, use your best verbal skills to reaffirm the goals and expectations you've charted. Clarify once more what the employee is to do to carry out the standards you've set for improving productivity, and

116

make it clear you're holding him or her responsible for doing what needs to be done to achieve the goals you've established. Put the standards you've agreed upon in writing, and note target dates for the completion of a project—or for each stage of a project.

Since some follow-up on your part will undoubtedly be needed to help the employee improve performance, let the employee know you'll be checking on his or her progress regularly. Follow through by observing changes for better or worse. To monitor and motivate, you may want to conduct informal performance appraisals on a continuing basis, and when the situation warrants it you might ask for regular progress reports from the subordinate.

As one more means of encouraging employees to achieve the set standards, show that you care about them and their professional growth and be available to provide any necessary counseling between performance appraisals.

Although the subject of raises doesn't always come up in performance appraisals, at some point you probably have to address requests for raises. Suppose, for example, a subordinate says, "Now that we've covered these other things, what can I expect in the way of a raise?"

Depending on the financial state of your company, you, as a manager, may have a specified amount of money allocated for raises. How you divide it among your staff depends on how important each employee is to the company and how effective his or her performance is.

If you plan to raise the salary of the person you're evaluating, you'd probably start your negotiations by suggesting the lowest possible amount you can conceivably offer—say 6 to 7 percent of the employee's present salary. You might say, "$1,400 more a year is what we think your raise should be." Your employee may respond, "I don't find that acceptable. A range of $1,800 to $1,900 is what I had in mind."

You realize the employee has asked for a sum that's higher than what he or she expects, so there's a good chance the person is mentally prepared to accept $1,700. Once you've determined

117

the bottom line the employee would consider adequate, you can delay a decision by saying you need more time to think about the request. Or, you can do some persuasive negotiating to lower the figure.

Try these verbal approaches to explain why you can't meet the employee's figure:

"You're one of the most important people on my staff. However, much as I would like to I can't give you the raise you deserve at this time because my budget for this department is tight, and we have to hold costs down."

"It's company policy that at your level I can't upgrade your salary beyond a certain percentage."

"The president of the corporation established the salary guidelines, and I can't go above the ceiling he sets."

You can also discuss employee benefits; emphasize the financial worth of the health plan, life insurance, pension system, profit-sharing program, and any other benefits.

If, after this initial approach, the employee is still not satisfied with the raise you've offered, negotiate an amount that's between your suggestion and his or her request. Even if you negotiate up a few hundred dollars—say, to $1,550—you're still below the amount asked for. And since the employee would have settled for $1,700, he or she may think, "Maybe I'd better take it. After all, it's not too far from what I hoped to settle for."

After the Appraisal

From *Briefings' Best Tips* come these two final tips:

First, be quick to recognize an employee who overcomes a deficiency or corrects a mistake. When you show this kind of interest, you help build morale.

Second, consider using an official "pat on the back" three-part form. Supervisors can easily and quickly write a line or two after an employee has done an outstanding job. Give the original to the employee, send a copy to the personnel file and retain a copy.[9]

If you apply every good verbal skill you've developed to giving performance appraisals, you'll keep the communication lines open between your staff and you. And you'll gain a feather in your corporate cap for effectively handling one of the most important jobs a manager does.

CHAPTER 11

A Manager's Performance Appraisal and Salary Review

"I want to get somewhere in this firm."

A manager is as likely to be the receiver as the giver of a performance appraisal. You can establish a solid record of achievements in the company if you use good verbal communication skills at your performance reviews. This is the case whether the appraisal is a formal one or simply a casual exchange.

You can enhance your corporate visibility by emphasizing your accomplishments and by seeking positive feedback on your achievements and potential. By the same token, you will be overlooked if you are so modest and quiet that you sell yourself short.

So how do you get your just rewards and heighten your

boss's reaction to even your smallest achievements? This chapter shows you how to develop the verbal skills to call attention to your performance.

Ask for Feedback

If there is no formal performance review at your company by which your boss gives you input on objectives and how well you're meeting them, ask for an informal review of your performance. "It's perfectly all right to do this," advises Dr. Donald Kirkpatrick, a management training and development consultant. "If you don't know what your boss expects and your boss doesn't take the initiative and tell you, you'd better take things in your own hands and go to him and find out."

For example, an assistant project manager in a large engineering firm was regarded by upper management as being laid back, satisfied with the job he'd held for five years. There were no reviews in his company, so no one ever asked him if he wanted to progress—or even bothered to evaluate if he had the potential.

Instead of lying low, the assistant decided to speak up. Taking matters into his own hands, he said to his supervisor, "You know, I want to get somewhere after five years in this firm, so I'd like a chance to talk with you about how you think I'm doing and what my potential is." The boss was so shocked at this revelation that he immediately responded, "But I didn't know you wanted to progress. I thought you seemed very happy doing what you've always done." When the shock was over, however, the boss set up a performance appraisal. In an hour-long session he went over the assistant's strengths and weaknesses and set forth the expectations he'd have if the assistant were promoted.

The assistant, in turn, emphasized his experience and provided his boss with an overall view of his career objectives. As a result of speaking up, the assistant progressed to a project manager's job when the first opportunity arose.

In his book *Rogers' Rules for Businesswomen* (and the same techniques apply to men!), Henry C. Rogers advocates that if your company has no formal review policy, you should ask your boss for informal performance reviews, possibly as frequently as every three months.[1]

To determine the proper time to approach your boss, Rogers suggests you study his work habits and determine when he is comparatively at ease and under the least amount of pressure. Ask yourself:

- Would this be in the early morning, when he is having his first cup of coffee?
- Is it after lunch, just before he gets into his afternoon work load?
- Is it at the end of the day, prior to leaving for home?

Once you pinpoint a time to approach your boss, ask for an appointment to discuss how you are doing. "Then have a string of questions ready for him," advises Rogers. He offers some you might consider asking:

1. Am I working up to your expectations for me?
2. Are we in agreement about what my priorities are?
3. Is there anything you would like me to do that I have not been doing?
4. Am I communicating with you satisfactorily, or is there room for improvement?
5. Do you mind if we have this conversation again three to six months from now?[2]

Prepare for Your Appraisal

Most large companies have a formal review process on a quarterly, semi-annual, or yearly basis. But, whether it's a formal or informal appraisal, first evaluate yourself—and document it in writing—before you go to your review.

Generally, you're most apt to use your documented self-evaluation and performance records at appraisal time. But it's advantageous to keep this information current throughout the entire year so that you have it on hand when a promotion opportunity arises. However, your evaluation and performance records are not something you should leave around or deliver to people when they don't ask for them. The most discreet means for circulating such information (except at appraisal time, when it automatically goes to the appropriate people) is to find a way to get people you want to see it to ask if you have something available. For example, a broadcasting executive puts a well-prepared list of what he has accomplished and what he would like to do in the inside pocket of his suit jacket whenever he attends a meeting or conference or goes out to a business meal. "Then, when someone starts talking about an opportunity somewhere in the organization that sounds as though it might fit what I've done or want to do, I mention—casually, at first—that I've been involved in that work and have many ideas about it.

"People kid me about my 'suit jacket' file, but often a colleague will speak up and say, 'Give me some of your thoughts when you have a chance.' That's when I pass out my record to someone I want to see it."

Another advantageous time to get a supervisor to look at your performance record is when you've done something especially good and are receiving kudos for it. When, as part of the kudos, a supervisor says, "I'm going to remember you as someone who gets right on a job," you can say, "Sometime when an opening arises I'd like to work on X project. I've kept a list of what I've done that's relevant to that project, so I'd welcome an appointment to discuss my ideas with you." If the reaction is positive, pull out your performance record for the supervisor to look over before you schedule an appointment.

Some companies have standard self-evaluation forms, though often managers forego the form and write their own performance records. Tony Cipollone of Metroweb Corporation explains how this works:

> We have self-evaluation forms for both managerial and supervisory personnel and hourly employees in our company.
>
> However, rather than using the form, I choose to write my own three- or four-page evaluation. As its format or basis, I use the objectives we set up the previous year as the things we intended to do ("Here's what we said last time") and my evaluation of whether or not those objectives were achieved ("Here is whether it was accomplished").
>
> Tying everything to that, I include in my total self-evaluation and performance record the following information:
>
> A list of my accomplishments
>
> The things that happened
>
> How these activities relate to the objectives we set forth
>
> The things that didn't occur that we decided to do last year
>
> What's going on now
>
> The direction I would like to go toward in the upcoming year
>
> Either the overall view of where I'm headed ties back into the previous objectives and says, "We didn't do 10 percent of what we wanted to see happen, so let's try to work on that 10 percent and add other objectives," or "Given what we know now I don't think we ought to go in that direction so let's move in this direction over here."

In Cipollone's company, he turns in his completed self-evaluation and performance record to his immediate supervisor.

Later, at a performance appraisal, the accomplishments, objectives, and priorities are discussed.

Although procedures for reviews vary with different companies, a conference between the immediate manager and the employee is standard practice. During the conference your performance record will be appraised. Occasionally issues that come out of the conference may be discussed by your immediate manager with a person at a higher level.

React Well to a Performance Appraisal

Chances are good that during the conference some aspect of your performance will receive a critical review. How you react to critical comments is crucial to your career. Here are five things to keep in mind.

1. *Acknowledge that you hear what your boss says.* Most managers believe the best verbal response is to acknowledge what is said and, when necessary, clarify what you hear with such phrases as "Do I understand you to mean? . . ."

When the appraisal is positive, if possible seize the opportunity to provide some specific ideas, information, and background on what you can do to expand on the positives.

On the other hand, if the review is negative, verify what you've heard so you're sure that what you think you heard is what was actually said. That way you understand exactly what the criticism is. Either ask such questions as, "What can be done to improve this?" or "How can I do it better?" Or, if answers are not immediately apparent, come to an agreement or set an agenda for working out the answers and doing things differently.

In some instances your supervisor may say something you strongly feel is wrong or misinformed. But even though you'd like to, you should not say bluntly, "You're the person who is wrong" or "You're off the wall with that information." Instead speak up tactfully with a phrase like, "With all due respect let me explain that I handled that situation as I did because the information I received (and verified with such sources as ————) indicated my decision was the best one for all of us at that time."

2. *Refrain from offering excuses when you respond to reprimands.* Suppose, in the midst of your appraisal, some minor shortcoming from the past is brought up—possibly a little event that irked your boss at the time. How do you deal with this? Cipollone offers some advice: "It's ineffective to offer excuses and weakly explain something away with, 'I was having a bad day' or whatever. . . . I'd just say, 'You're right.' "

"*Never* offer excuses," adds Milo Sobel, a management educator and expert in communication. "An excuse implies that you're not wrong, even though you may be *dead* wrong, so it's much better for a manager to say:

'I was wrong—I don't have an excuse.'

'I can offer you an explanation if you want to hear it, but I still feel badly that I'm wrong.'

'I accept responsibility and have no excuse.'

'You have a right to feel the way you do.'

'I'm sorry.'

'Can I make it up to you in any way?' "

Sobel recalls an incident in his earlier employment, when he didn't leave home in enough time to allow for his train being late. "I arrived at my office at 9:25 instead of shortly before 9:00—and the phones were ringing off the hook. Normally three of us would be working in my office area at that time, but that particular day was one of those weird ones when the other two people weren't there to field the ringing phones."

The situation irked Sobel's boss and put him in an awkward spot. But when the reprimand came up, Sobel's verbal approach was to say: "I was wrong. I don't have an excuse. If you want an explanation I can give you one, but it's still not good enough—and I'm still wrong. All I can say is I would never knowingly do anything to embarrass you, and I'll do all I can to make sure it never happens again."

Sobel points out that "You don't have to volunteer an explanation, but if the other person wants to know why, you can offer one. An explanation implies that you know you're wrong—as opposed to excuses which, as I said, simply imply you think you're not wrong. Most people admire you when you're willing to take your own lumps," he concludes, "so don't let yourself off the hook. Let someone else let you off the hook instead."

3. *Avoid being defensive.* Your situation is much more serious when a mistake is recorded in your job file. If this is the case, be well prepared with a good verbal response, should someone refer to the mistake. "You can't whitewash and downplay a mistake or say, 'I want to forget about that,' " advises Cipollone.

Instead, know how the mistake happened, acknowledge it, and—(as in shunning excuses)—say, "Yes, that happened and it was a mistake. It was not an appropriate thing to do, and I see now, if I didn't see it before, that it could have been done in a different way."

Next, emphasize, "Here's what I learned from it and what I'll do differently if a similar situation occurs." Or, "Here's what good will now come out of it." "Here's why, maybe, it wasn't so bad that it happened, because of what I learned."

As we previously discussed, there may be times when a criticism is totally unjustified and when a mistake is erroneously recorded in your file. Understandably you want to be hostile and defensive in those situations. But take a moment to calm yourself. Then point out firmly that the recorded error does not legitimately belong in your file. Say, "When I explain why it shouldn't be there, I'm sure you will understand and agree."

Cipollone suggests that your responses be verbal only. "I personally don't think you should add a note of your own to your file explaining the mistake away or putting your own perspective on it. To me, that's not a good signal because it says so clearly, 'This guy is on the defensive and doesn't know enough to admit a mistake.' I think you have to leave it up to the discretion and good judgment of the person seeing it in the file to put it in context and talk to you about it.''

Also, Cipollone points out that if you've already talked to your immediate boss, or whoever put it in your file in the first place, and said that it was a mistake and that you've learned from it, the person reviewing the file can talk to your immediate boss. Your boss can then provide the background for you; if you've responded well to your immediate boss, the situation can even come out positive.

4. *Highlight your potential for increased responsibility.* Just as the assistant project manager in the engineering firm discovered, there's no better opportunity than at review time to ask for greater responsibility—especially if you're aware of a company problem for which you might have a solution.

For example, if the person in charge of handling that problem is wondering what to do about it, you might suggest your approach and ask to join the task force working on it, even if the problem is not in your area of responsibility. Try saying, "I see this problem, and I have some ideas on how we might solve it."

You can also use these other approaches:

"Since I handled thus-and-so, how about letting me try something different or something more that would build on it?"

"Here's something I've uncovered in my work, and I have a proposal on how I could do something with it."

"Here is an area that, it seems to me, could really help us out if we could explore it and do something with it. Do you agree?"

5. *Accept praise graciously.* Too often people downplay praise with, "Oh, it wasn't such a big deal" or some other dismissal. But people who give compliments like the praise to

be appreciated. When you're on the receiving end, don't down-play it. Instead, acknowledge and accept the praise with a phrase as simple as thank-you.

"If someone says, 'That was great work you did on that project' and you respond, 'It wasn't anything really,' you're subtly putting that person down and indicating he can't judge good work," explains Tony Cipollone. "The same thing is true if a person says, 'That's a nice suit' and you answer, 'Oh, this old thing—I've had it for years.' What you've just done is to put down the other person for not recognizing that this is an old out-of-style garment. You've subtly insulted him for thinking it was a nice thing."

Naturally, how you respond to praise depends on the situation. Along with such simple comments as, "I'm glad you like it," "Glad it helped you out," or something to the effect of, "I heard your praise and I'm glad you gave it to me," a thank-you is sufficient. It's unnecessary to downplay or embellish either what you did or why you did it.

Negotiate a Raise

When your performance review is positive and you have accomplishments to highlight, speak up and request a raise if the person reviewing your work doesn't bring it up first. (Of course, if your company policy requires that raise negotiations be discussed at a separate meeting, it's probably best to follow the rules.) Many managers recommend not quoting a specific figure at the start of a money discussion, lest you name a figure lower than you might otherwise be offered. As in any negotiation, avoid showing your hand. But let's look at the process in stages.

Preparation

For an effective negotiation, plan your strategy ahead of time. Then you can go to your appraisal armed with information, including a written record of your duties, responsibilities, skills, and achievements.

Assemble a record of how your responsibilities have increased and what you do—and have done—that are over and above your regular job. Sometimes it's appropriate to look at the results your supervisor has achieved and relate that to how you've assisted in that progress. In addition, put yourself in your boss's shoes and think of the reasons he would like to hear for negotiating the increase you want. Ask yourself, "What does my boss need that he or she wouldn't have without me?"

Size of the Raise

When it's time to talk money, many employers use your present salary as a negotiating base. But for the base you want to start at, be prepared with current information. Check on how your company is doing (whether its profits are large or small) by reading its annual report and talking to people who are "in the know." Also, determine what you're worth in the job market. For example, research your value in dollars by getting up-to-the-minute salary information for the work you do. Find out what others doing the same work are earning, and check compensation surveys published by your trade association or professional organization. Then use this information to determine the size of raise you can justify.

"Once you know the realistic range of your market value, you need to determine whether you're a person in relatively short supply before you go pushing beyond that range," advises Dr. David Eyler, program manager of a private educational project.

If you're a relatively common administrative-type manager who is not in short supply, you're a little crazy to try to go beyond normal expectations. On the other hand, if you're a red-hot something and a manager in an area for which there's a high demand, you can articulate that. In this situation, if you have a good track record and there aren't a lot of people waiting in line to do the same thing, you can ask for more.

Arguments for the Raise

All requests for raises should be tied to your job and why you deserve more money. Your arguments should be based on merit, performance, production, and the demands of the job. Keeping that in mind, it's inappropriate to include anything personal, such as, "I need more money because of my personal situation." Most employers are not persuaded by arguments such as:

"I need a new car."

"I'm going to buy a house."

"I have a large family to support."

As Tony Cipollone points out, "A representative of the company can sympathize with [these pleas] but [they aren't] a valid argument for giving a manager more money.

The person negotiating the raise has to consider the company at large, so he is going to think, "If I do this for you, here are other people in the same category. What am I going to do then? If I pay based on the fact that you have eight children and someone else has two—that's not job or performance related. It's not appropriate."
Even saying you need money because of [a higher] cost of living is not really appropriate or job-related, because presumably the cost of living is tied into the salary structure and everyone has this problem.

Though every supervisor makes it clear that a raise ought not to be connected with a need for more money, Cipollone adds the pertinent point that *needing* and *wanting* are different. "If wanting is connected to the marketplace—for example,

'Other people in this type of job make X dollars, so it seems as though I ought to make X dollars too'—that's a more appropriate approach, and management can understand that kind of thinking.''

Possible Responses

One possible reaction your supervisor might have to your raise request is that although he can make salary recommendations, he is powerless on the final decision. Should that happen, ask who has the power. See if your supervisor will support your request to that person.

Another frequent reaction is, "Other people are doing good jobs too, and they're not receiving the kind of raise you're seeking." In that situation, Sherry Chastain, author of *Winning the Salary Game,* advocates looking the employer squarely in the eye and saying nothing. "That's their problem, not yours," she notes. "But if you can't handle that tactic, say 'I'm only talking about myself.' ''[3]

Similarly, if your employer offers a sum that's far below what you want, Chastain suggests looking dismayed and remaining silent. "By consciously initiating the silence and sticking to it," she says, "odds are the employer will come back with a better offer or at least encourage further negotiating."[4]

If, despite your best planning and presentation, your boss stays firm on the size of your raise and there's no way to get the figure you want at appraisal time, consider saying, "Okay, I'm willing to work at the salary you're offering now, if we have an understanding that in three months we'll have a review of my accomplishments and progress." Ask for a definite time to renegotiate. Let it be known that, with the raise you deserve, you'll continue to serve the best interests of the company. And follow up all raise negotiations with a memo that recaps your understanding.

CHAPTER 12

Offering Criticism

"Now that you know about it, I'm sure it won't happen again."

Criticism is a reality in the corporate world, and the way you give it can be an essential factor in showcasing your promotion potential.

Unfortunately, many managers are unable to criticize well, despite the fact that few things cause as much conflict as harsh criticism. In fact, as Daniel Goleman wrote in *The New York Times,* "Of all the touchy moments on the job, an exchange of criticism ranks high on the list. Most everyone dislikes being criticized and many people are reluctant to offer it, especially to colleagues."[1]

In studies conducted by Dr. Robert Baron, a psychologist at Rensselaer Polytechnic Institute, it was established that volunteers who'd received harsh negative criticism were unlikely to cooperate in the future with the person who gave the criticism. Many participants in the study also indicated they wanted to avoid future contact altogether. And the criticism, according to Baron, so demoralized those who received it that they no longer tried as hard at their work and no longer felt as able to perform.[2]

Despite these normal negative reactions, however, criticism can be positive. When managers give it effectively, it can be the genesis of a healthy relationship as well as a way of providing constructive and considerate help.

When Is Criticism in Order?

Generally, criticism is valid when the people you manage aren't functioning well. It's equally justifiable when you sincerely want to help them improve or upgrade their performance, change a harmful behavior pattern, or resolve a situation that's threatening your working relationship.

Regardless of the reason, though, it's important first to think through exactly what you're going to say and how you're going to say it. This planning will give you a fighting chance to have the criticism accepted.

Although responses to criticism vary with persons and circumstances, Dr. Clifford Swensen, professor of psychological sciences at Purdue University, advises that usually you can expect one of four reactions:

1. People may become hostile and defend themselves, and attack you because they resent and reject the criticism.
2. They may point out how the criticism is based on misunderstanding or error, and say, "That isn't the way it happened. That isn't what I did. That isn't what I intended."
3. They may indicate they were unaware of the problem, and say, "I didn't know about that" or "That never occurred to me, and I really don't think that's the way I react. But I'll give it some thought and see whether or not there's truth to it."
4. They may agree with you and say, "Yes, you're right, and I should change my way of doing things."

Depending on how well—or how poorly—you offer your criticism, you can anticipate and prepare for each of these

134

responses. But the possibility of a positive response is more likely if you score well on the following quiz. Check the responses that apply to you and score yourself at the end.

	A Always	B Sometimes	C Never
1. Do you proceed with caution, trying to understand why another person's behavior bothers you before you criticize?	___	___	___
2. Do you refrain from blurting out what's on your mind, without asking yourself how much your words may hurt?	___	___	___
3. Do you avoid putting people on the defensive, trying not to lash out in a hostile, accusatory way with too much frankness and unmeasured honesty?	___	___	___
4. Do you focus on what people do well and approach negatives in constructive ways as you seek to improve a relationship or help someone change a harmful behavior?	___	___	___

	A Always	B Sometimes	C Never
5. Do you suggest positive and beneficial solutions to the behavior you criticize?	____	____	____
6. Do you avoid criticizing others when you're angry, overtired, or frustrated—or when things seem to be going better for them than for you?	____	____	____
7. Do you hold back from being critical when you see traits in others you don't like in yourself—or behavior patterns your parents had that always bothered you?	____	____	____
8. Do you choose a quiet place to offer criticism, a place where there is little risk of other people overhearing your conversation?	____	____	____
9. Do you avoid putting people down when they feel worthless, hopeless, and useless?	____	____	____

	A Always	B Sometimes	C Never
10. Do you offer the criticism as soon as possible after a troublesome incident?	____	____	____
11. Do you speak in a concrete, tactful way and avoid generalizations?	____	____	____
12. Do you limit the length of your criticism and avoid rambling on?	____	____	____
TOTALS	____	____	____

Scoring: Add up your A, B, and C answers. If the majority are A's, you're handling criticism in an effective way. But if your score is mostly B's and C's (or overwhelmingly C's), you need to sharpen your criticism skills.

Twelve Ways to Criticize Effectively

Here are twelve ways to build your verbal skills for giving criticism more effectively.

1. *Examine your need to criticize.* Look at whether you're seeking to improve a situation or you're just expressing your own frustrations. For example, "Often in counseling I see relationships in which one person is more successful than the

other," explains Lynne Bergman, a Westwood, New Jersey–based therapist. "When the less successful person feels frustration because things are going better for others, there can be subconscious angers or jealousies. Thus it's important to recognize how much of what we want to criticize has to do with us and how much has to do with the other person."

2. *Ease into the criticism.* Sometimes, it's helpful to ask other people if they'd like to hear how you feel about what they're doing. Dr. Harriet Lefkowith, a human resources development specialist who leads workshops on communication, suggests, "You can begin with, 'I think it's important for me to tell you what it is that's getting in the way of our relationship.' When you describe your feelings instead of blaming another person's actions, you don't trigger defenses."

When using your feelings as a means of easing into criticism, however, avoid making people feel self-conscious or threatening their self-esteem. As Lefkowith suggests, couch the feedback in terms of your perception: "I have a problem, and I'd like to discuss it with you. I'm having some negative feelings about things you're doing. May I give you some feedback about it and tell you how I feel?"

And when giving feedback, don't be judgmental, putting labels on people's actions. For example, rather than saying, "You always push the panic button," describe how that person's habit affects you as a manager. Avoid citing the behavior as a mark of character or implying it represents a flaw in the other person.

"A character attack—calling someone stupid or incompetent—misses the point," advises Dr. J. R. Larson, a psychologist at the University of Illinois, whose studies were also reported in Daniel Goleman's *New York Times* article. "You immediately put him on the defensive so that he's no longer receptive to what you have to tell him about how to do things better."[3]

3. *Weigh the consequences before you speak.* It's always wise to measure the risk-benefit ratio of your criticism. Assess the personality of the individual you're about to criticize. If your

staff, co-workers, or supervisors never see criticism as constructive, you'll risk future difficulties because these people will want to get back at you. For example, Ted, a real estate managing agent, hired Jack, an assistant manager, to be his right-hand man. But they both got on the defensive and upset their relationship when Ted called in Jack and demanded a file on a new condo listing. "But, Ted, you know that file isn't ready!" Jack responded in frustration. "You told me yourself to hold up on it till we have all the data we need."

"That isn't true," Ted exclaimed. "You never listen to what I say, so you've made a *big* mistake."

"You're the one who makes mistakes," Jack retorted angrily. "You're always forgetting what you say. This is the *third* time you've done it." A heated argument followed, and Ted, in order to get back at Jack, placed Jack's managerial rise on hold. He set him up for failure and placed him in situations where every error he made would be noticed by top management.

Ted's managerial style of demanding instead of requesting could certainly use some refinement. Nevertheless, Ted was the boss, and he also had a reputation for never taking criticism well. Jack should have been aware of this and tempered his manner, tone, and words so they were less accusatory. A more mellow "The file isn't ready yet. Remember how we both agreed. . . ." might have prevented an argument and the harsh consequences for Jack.

4. *Choose the right place.* If you can possibly avoid it, never criticize someone in front of others.

Admittedly—and realistically—companies would grind to a halt if managers always waited to be alone with a person when called on to criticize. But when possible and practical, say, "There's something I need to discuss with you, so what would be a good time for us to be uninterrupted?"

"One of the most mortifying moments of my life was when my manager, with his door wide open, criticized one of the room designs that I had put together," explains Karen, an assistant manager in a furniture gallery. "I couldn't focus on anything except my overwhelming discomfort as people I worked with walked by the door and heard what he said to me.''

5. *Choose the right time.* In the University of Illinois studies, Dr. J. R. Larson found that one of the most common problems in the delivery of criticism is timing:

> Too often it is long delayed, and such a lag may have unintended consequences. Most problems in an employee's performance are not sudden. They develop slowly over time. When the boss fails to let his feelings be known promptly it leads to his frustration building up slowly. Then one day he blows up about it. If the criticism had been given earlier on, the employee would have been able to correct the problem.[4]

To this Dr. Baron has added, "Too often people criticize only when things boil over, when they get too angry to contain themselves."[5] When this occurs, Baron has found, they give the criticism in the worst way: in biting sarcasm, threats, and a long list of the grievances they had kept to themselves. Such attacks invariably backfire, however. Since they're received as an affront to one's dignity, the recipient becomes angry in return. It's the worst way to motivate someone.

6. *Substantiate your criticism.* While an assistant in a large investigative agency was out of the office, the manager of the agency noticed some confidential files spread out on the assistant's desk. When the manager called the assistant to his office, his documented approach began with, "I saw some credit history papers spread out on your desk. You and I know these confidential matters must not be out in plain view. I'm sure that this was an oversight, but I find it extremely upsetting because it tells me that unintentionally you're growing a little careless with confidential matters. Now that you know about it, though, I'm sure it won't happen again."

Expressed in this manner and given in a straightforward way, the criticism provided the assistant with a chance to respond to the accuracy of the statement. By the same token, it encouraged an explanation, reduced defensiveness, and gave the assistant a chance to do things differently the next time.

7. *Approach people in a friendly way*. The research on criticism has shown that people respond best when critiques are delivered in a considerate, sensitive, and direct manner. Therefore, use eye contact and be careful with your tone of voice. Choose your words carefully and avoid expressions like, "You always," "You never," and "You should." These phrases are viewed as attacks and they put other people on the defensive.

Similarly, avoid teasing, casting your criticism in terms of a joke, or aiming your remarks indirectly. "When you tease, joke, or act indirect, you make people wonder about the level of your relationship since you can't be straight with them," says Lynne Bergman. "But when you speak in a direct way, your criticism is taken as concern coming from an adult who has something to say."

8. *Concentrate on behavior, not personality*. Make it clear that you respect the other person. Depersonalize the criticism; in other words, separate the person from the behavior. You can begin with, "I'm not criticizing you as a person, but a certain behavior disturbs me. I'm saying this to help our relationship, to keep you out of trouble, to improve your performance. . . ."

Dr. Harriet Lefkowith offers an example:

If an assistant has a behavior that's offensive to you—say she's not getting her work out on time—that doesn't mean that she herself is offensive or a late or lazy person. She may be a very good worker and do everything well, but she's tardy in getting her reports to her team head, so give her feedback on that situation rather than saying "You're always late." She's apt to respond to the latter, "So you think I'm always late! Was I late on Tuesday?" Then you're talking about Tuesday instead of the fact that when she is late she's holding up the entire team in finishing the monthly report on time. You're speaking to her in a descriptive way, not a personally evaluative way.

9. *Be specific*. Precise communication turns a critique into an opportunity for improvement. Communication experts stress

that criticism with concrete examples helps people focus on what you're talking about. As Dr. Baron has noted,

> Constructive criticism tells you exactly what you did wrong, instead of just being a cryptic and vague attack. If someone tells you you're doing wrong, but doesn't say just how, it's utterly demoralizing. It undermines your confidence.[6]

10. *Combine compliments with criticism*. In his studies, Dr. Larson found that many managers are frugal with their praise while generous with their criticism.

> Some people have as much trouble with praise as with criticism. Unless it's an outstanding job, they don't say anything. But if you do a bad job, they're ready to let you know it. People often tell me that they don't hear much from their boss about how they're doing until there's a mistake.[7]

When you feel you must criticize a person for a mistake or a poorly executed job—or maybe an offensive behavior—give a compliment first to soften the criticism and make it easier to hear and accept your comments. "But be sure it's a sincere compliment," points out Lynne Bergman, "because if it's not sincere, the other person will not believe it's intended in a constructive way."

For example, Walter, a manager in a resort hotel, was convinced that Bill, an assistant whom he had had for six months, was one of the smartest, most enthusiastic young managers he had ever met. Bill was brilliant and personable in every possible way, except for his troublesome habit of interrupting people who were speaking and then saying irrelevant things. This habit was disturbing, but in order to preserve their relationship Walter criticized Bill by first complimenting him on his great personality. Then he specifically pointed out how Bill recently overstepped his bounds.

"Yesterday at lunch you were by far the greatest and most informed conversationalist at the table," said Walter in a light, friendly tone. "But I'm concerned that because you're so articulate the rest of us don't have a chance to finish the sentences we start. We can't all be as brilliant as you—but why not give us a try?" The criticism was received well.

11. *Criticize only what can be changed.* "To criticize behavior, mannerisms, and characteristics that can't be changed is a dead-end street," warns Harriet Lefkowith. "It may get something off your chest, but the person is left with the feeling, 'What am I supposed to do?' "

Take the case of Martin, an assistant in an accounting firm, who had a raspy cough. None of the doctors he had seen had been able to find the root of his trouble, so Martin continued to clear his throat and cough in the office. His cough grated on the head accountant's nerves, particularly when he was having a difficult day. On one hassle-filled day, the accountant snapped at Martin, "Why don't you try to stop coughing!" After this thoughtless criticism the accountant walked away. But no amount of trying could help Martin, so he became only more self-conscious every time he had to cough.

12. *Concentrate on one criticism at a time.* It's important to call attention to only one objectionable behavior at a time, rather than to drag up grievances from the past. The latter are bound to antagonize and are after the fact.

Sometimes this approach can make enemies, too. For example, a lawyer in a corporation criticized a young assistant for unwittingly overlooking a fact in his research. After criticizing the assistant for the current oversight, the lawyer kept lashing out, recalling every mistake the assistant had made in his two years with the firm. The assistant, in turn, was so enraged by the nonstop attack that he asked for an immediate transfer. Though he remained with the corporation and moved up through the ranks, he refused ever again to speak to or deal with that particular attorney.

A better verbal approach for the lawyer would have been to stick with the current oversight and ask, "Was there a reason why you didn't include this fact?" This question would have given the assistant a chance to explain. "In almost every situation, if several things bother you, you refrain from mentioning them simultaneously," adds Lynne Bergman. "Pick the most relevant item that troubles you and see that you stick with that."

The task of criticizing others will never be the favorite job of most managers. But it comes with the territory, as the saying goes, and must be done. When you're able to do it effectively—with good verbal skills—you'll help your staff members improve their performances or change harmful behavior patterns. Always remember to think through first not only what you're going to say but how you're going to say it.

CHAPTER 13

Receiving Criticism

*"Let's wait until we both get all the facts before
we continue."*

As studies on criticism show, many people end up with destructive emotions after having received criticism. Thus, in order to cope with it effectively, managers must have strong verbal skills when they are the receivers. In Chapter 12, we discussed Dr. Robert Baron's studies on criticism at Rensselaer Polytechnic Institute. Dr. Baron found that among 108 managers and white-collar workers, the poor handling of criticism was one of the top five causes of work conflicts. And in this group of five causes, criticism ranked higher than mistrust, conflicting personalities, and disputes over power and pay.[1]

In another of his studies Dr. Baron had volunteers take part in a simulation in which one person was asked to come up with an advertising campaign for a new shampoo. Another "volunteer" (actually Dr. Baron's accomplice) then evaluated the ideas.

Each volunteer received one of two critiques—either the remarks were considerate and specific, or the criticism was inconsiderate and blamed the person's innate deficiencies for the problem. The latter critique included such comments as:

"Didn't even try."

"Can't seem to do anything right."

"I'll try to get someone else to do it."

The recipients' emotions ran the gamut from anger to tension. And this experiment revealed, as had other studies, that even a single, inept criticism can have a devastating effect on a person's morale and can directly impair his or her ability to work effectively.[2]

"It's understandably human to see criticism as a painful put-down, and invariably most people do react negatively to it," points out Dr. Harriet Lefkowith, a human resources development specialist. "Before you know it, the act of criticism turns into an armed camp with two sides. Nobody's thinking. There's no problem solving. Everyone's defending him or her self."

Stand Up to Criticism

One woman on the losing side of that armed camp was a new copywriter in a direct mail organization. She came to the job straight from college, so she had no experience in standing up to criticism from an emotional, irrational boss. The copywriter was assigned to one phase of a job on her boss's team, but because she did not understand her boss's erratic directions, innumerable things went wrong.

Her boss criticized her bitterly every time she slipped up. Though the young woman was shaken by what he said, she made every effort to do what he asked. But criticizing her privately was not enough for him. In a meeting of the entire team, he cited the copywriter as "one horrifying example" of how things shouldn't be done.

The copywriter had no idea how to respond, or how to receive the insensitive words. She quit and found a job with future. But you can't quit your job every time you're criticized—

or waste your energy and time by taking everything personally. You don't want to put your ego on the line with every critical word aimed at you.

A manager needs to stand up to critics in a positive and straightforward way. You must learn to respond well verbally, to show yourself as a person with upper-management potential, rather than someone who falls apart as the copywriter did.

Here is a two-step program for achieving the verbal agility to stand up to your critics.

1. *Examine why and when your colleagues are likely to criticize you.* To cope with present and future criticism, you need to (1) evaluate the motives and credibility of your critics, (2) recognize whether their criticism is rational or emotional, (3) decide whether they're trying to hurt or help you, and (4) determine whether they have anything to gain by putting you down.

You often will receive valid criticism from a senior executive who sincerely wants to help you develop to your full potential. Sometimes, though, you may be the butt of unjust criticism for any number of reasons. For example, Dr. Clifford Swensen, professor of psychological sciences at Purdue University, points out that people criticize others for traits they don't like in themselves. They also criticize when they see behaviors they disliked in their parents. "People are inclined to be highly sensitive to these faults," stresses Swensen.

Because there are so many reasons why people will be overly critical of you or fault you unfairly for something, it's important you determine why they act as they do. Once you know (as opposed to presume) the dynamics involved, you can deal with their criticism more effectively.

When the criticism isn't valid, it is likely to be motivated by the following:

1. Your critics are hiding some anxiety, anger, disappointment, fear, hurt, confusion, or vulnerability themselves.

Their critical behavior is often a cover-up for their own frustrations and the pressures they feel.

2. Your critics may feel defensive and inferior. They have an ongoing compulsion to put others on the defensive, too, in order to appear important themselves.

3. Your critics have a strong sense of the way that others should behave. They think they are always in the right, and are self-appointed authorities on what people should do and be.

2. *Take charge of your critics before they take charge of you.* Get the upper hand on your critics and be ready for their remarks.

As a first step, draw a line down the middle of a piece of paper. On one side write the names of the people most apt to criticize you. On the other side, list why and when they might berate you. For example:

Person	*Why or When*
Barry	He's frustrated with his own job progress. Criticizes at every opportunity.
Jeanette	She's insecure about her position. If I mention a raise to George while we're talking informally at lunch, she'll think I'm going over her head.
Fred	He's a know-it-all. He's looking for a way to get back at me because of our disagreement over the land purchase proposal.

Strategies for Calming Your Critics

Now that you've determined the reasons behind the criticism you receive, plan to calm and subdue your critics with the following three verbal strategies. Inasmuch as your critics will expect an immediate argument from you, these strategies can temper their criticism and throw them off balance.

1. *Use appropriate humor, in moderate doses*. In some situations, you can simply acknowledge a fact. Without giving any ground, you can respond to a criticism in an amiable, disarming way by injecting a little humor.

"Everything is in how you respond," says Doe Lang, author of *The Secret of Charisma: What It Is and How to Get It* (New Choices Press). "Suppose, for example, someone says, 'You look defensive about this.' You might answer in a light tone, laughing, 'I guess you're right, but I'm not at my best when someone attacks me.' "

2. *Delay the attack.* Generally speaking, it's wise to bide your time until the critic loses momentum. Then you can respond to most criticism with a rational discussion that could not be achieved when a critic is in a harsh mood.

In other situations, your own harsh response may occasionally quiet a critic. But mostly a harsh response causes a critic to open fire on you, letting loose with even more criticism in an artless verbal spurt. Granted, you can't let demeaning words just slip by while you stall for time. You want to make sure your demeanor shows you know what your critic is saying and that you're not backing off from his or her words. But most criticism needn't be answered at once. Though your ego is involved, wait to respond.

You can often slow down your critic by calmly suggesting that you make an appointment to continue the talk later. For example,

> "Let's talk about this when you're not upset. When's a good time for you?"

> "I really don't think that's the way I react, but I'd like to think about it and then get back to you."

> "I'm sure we can discuss this much more productively when the shouting is over and we have uninterrupted time together."

> "Let's wait till we both get all the facts before we continue this."

149

3. *Listen to the criticism.* Pay close attention to how your critic perceives the problem. If you can't halt the attack or stall for time, carefully listen to the grievances. Even if the comments are unjust, use the listening skills described in Chapter 4. It's a good management tool.

By studying your critic's perception of the situation, often you can work down to the underlying problem and get closer to a solution with minimal agitation. If any of the criticism is justified, express your interest in finding a solution and indicate a willingness to negotiate when necessary. For example, you might say, "I'm glad you're saying what's on your mind. Actually, I haven't considered my views or behavior in that light. Let me think about it."

When you're faced with a critic who uses barbed humor or teasing instead of bringing the criticism into the open, confront the person with a comment such as, "I gather you don't agree with me. Would you like to talk about it?"

These indirect critics likely will back away from the directness of your approach as well as the criticism they tried to veil. But however they react, you've made it clear that you have seen through their ploy and recognize the message they have sent.

PART III

Take Control of Negative Situations

CHAPTER 14

Conflicts and Confrontations

"Perhaps we can find a solution that will satisfy both of us."

In addition to being peopled with critics, the corporate world is staffed with executives and co-workers who make your heart pound and your blood boil when they confront you with their verbal attacks.

The touch-and-go crises these attacks cause can disrupt a manager's day and bring out the worst in those who are working to get ahead. But the managers who keep their cool under fire and speak up effectively are the men and women who earn the respect of others and eventually realize their career potential.

Who Are the Antagonists?

Just as you wrote down the names of the people most apt to criticize you, and why and when they're likely to do it, you'll find that the first step in resolving other corporate conflicts is to

153

identify problem people—those who have the potential of upsetting you to the point that you're unable to do your best work.

The following is a list of personality traits. They describe the most common problem people in the corporate world.

Whose names will you use to fill in the blanks?

Abrasive_____

Abusive_____

Arrogant_____

Browbeating_____

Condescending_____

Demeaning_____

Disagreeable_____

Disconcerting_____

Domineering_____

Egotistical_____

Impatient_____

Impossible_____

Irrational_____

Obnoxious_____

Overbearing_____

Patronizing_____

Phoney_____

Pompous_____

Sarcastic_____

Tyrannical_____

Unreasonable_____

Now that you've identified these corporate bullies, consider why they bother you so much. For example, in a series of interviews, I asked managers to identify the problems that corporate bullies cause. I heard these statements again and again:

"They antagonize, rattle, or intimidate you."

"They embarrass and humiliate you in front of others."

"They fly off the handle and say things that should never be said."

"They upstage you and steal the credit that should be given to you."

"They frustrate and confuse you."

"They ignore and overlook you."

"They keep you on the defensive."

"They demoralize you and wound your pride."

"They constantly check on what you're doing and ask why you're doing it that way."

"They make you feel like a nothing."

Five Ways to Resolve Conflicts

There isn't any one right way to respond to a confrontation, but the following approaches can minimize the conflicts that problem people cause.

1. *Analyze the confrontations you've had with others in the past.* See if there's a pattern. To do this, write in-depth answers to the following questions:

- What really happened in the confrontations you have had with others?
- When have these confrontations occurred?
- How have you been dealing with the conflicts in the past?
- What kind of conflicts have other people had with these people?
- What do you think have been the motives behind these confrontations?

- What allowances have you made for the other person's human frailities?
- What have been your expectations as to how people should react to your ideas and actions?
- Have you tried to anticipate the words, actions, and attitudes that have thrown you off and disturbed your relationships?

2. *Give explanations rather than excuses.* It's human to want to strike right back with a defensive excuse—especially if, for example, your boss explodes when you make a decision that's wrong in his book of rules. But if you have a good reason for making a decision, it's smarter to create the impression that you're on equal ground.

For example, Pete, a team member in an architectural firm, decided to bend a company rule and send blueprints to a client before the department head, Tom, had approved them. When a furious Tom attacked Pete for acting on his own, Pete's first reaction was to make excuses and then to eat humble pie. But soon he gathered his forces and met Tom head on with, "Look, Tom, I'd like to explain this action and why I had to act quickly to save the company's face. Can I see you in your office later this afternoon?"

3. *Work on equal grounds with outside consultants and vendors.* Many consultants and vendors are a pleasure to work with, but others are confrontational. They can throw you off track or intimidate you if you let them dominate you with their do-it-my-way approach. They tend to discount your needs and disagree with the way you like to do things. But you can turn the tables and avoid confrontations with these people.

Let's say, for example, that your boss brings in an outside consultant to review your office's procedures. The consultant will then revamp and upgrade the systems to increase productivity.

The consultant pushes you hard to change your filing system, but you know from ten years' experience that the present system works. You see no reason to change. You need to maintain a good relationship with the consultant, but he grates on your nerves with his steady, "This will have to go."

How do you speak up tactfully while avoiding a conflict? Sometimes it's effective simply to sit there and nod your head, even though you don't plan to put into effect what the consultant recommends. Rather than cause a clash, you listen to what he has to say and, in turn, suggest he give you more specific ideas on how to make best use of his suggestions. You know you won't follow them, but he doesn't have to know that. Through this pacifying approach, you can minimize his confrontational manner. Try using such expressions as:

"What suggestions for implementation do you have?"

"I'm willing to give what you say some thought."

"Give me some time to think over what you say so we can see how to approach it."

As an alternative to this false "yes-ing," you can say "No" graciously (but firmly) to the confrontational consultant who comes to you with a set program. In most instances, it will help if right from the beginning you have laid your needs out on the table by saying, "This is the problem we have to resolve" or "This is what would be useful to us." But sometimes, even when you do this, certain consultants will still try to make an inflexible program fit every circumstance. When this happens tell the consultant "No" by stating, "I understand what you're trying to show us, but in our particular situation it's inappropriate." Then be prepared to explain to whoever hired the consultant why the consultant's ideas would not have worked.

Vendors are the people a company depends upon for services and supplies, but how does a manager get what he or she wants from them without creating conflicts?

In one case, the quality control manager for a manufacturer of electrical panelboards and switchboards was having problems with the quality of the materials his company was getting from a supplier with whom it had a contract. Moreover, some deliveries

157

were arriving so late that manufacturing was being delayed. In turn, sales representatives were losing customers because the manufacturer was unable to ship orders on time.

It was essential for the manager to work out the crisis at once. But she knew from previous experience that the verbal attack she'd like to use on the offending vendor would create a confrontation. She couldn't risk a conflict that might make things worse, so after meeting with the managers in purchasing and sales she approached the vendor calmly with:

"The problem we're facing is this. . . ." Let's work it out together."

"What ideas do you have for straightening out this situation?"

"Can we agree on a new shipping plan that will prevent late deliveries in the future?"

"Now that we've worked out these wrinkles we'll be expecting top-grade material on the promised delivery dates."

4. *Compromise and negotiate.* Effective methods of resolving conflicts are (1) conceding and compromising a point without losing ground, (2) proposing a solution to satisfy both parties, (3) suggesting an alternative action, and (4) negotiating an exchange of favors. Each of these methods is designed to enable both persons to win.

"In many situations it's a matter of saving face for everyone involved," explains Dr. David Eyler, who manages a large educational project:

In some situations you can indicate you're prepared to make certain changes and considerations if the other person is. In others, you can let everyone come out with a piece of the action—or the prospect of getting a piece next time.

Also, when you can't offer them anything this time

158

around, you can sometimes keep them from denying you something by your tone of voice—and the tone of the conversation—indicating that you are going to support them when something else comes around.

Some expressions to use when working out a compromise are:

"If you'll support me in this expenditure, I'll stand behind you on your budget when that comes up for approval."

"Some alternatives are worth trying."

"Perhaps we can find a solution that will satisfy both of us."

"What do you think a fair solution would be?"

"How would you like me to handle this?"

When negotiating a compromise, avoid distancing expressions such as, "Yes, but." These phrases are guaranteed to reduce your chances of a successful compromise. Above all, end your negotiation on a positive note, with a realistic optimism that shows you're in control.

5. *Plan ahead*. Always prepare for a confrontation so you can speak up effectively, in a way that will lessen the impact of the conflict.

Suppose, for example, that you are Pete, the team member mentioned earlier as severely chastised by Tom, his department head. Pete had bypassed corporate protocol and acted on his own, so he asked for a meeting with Tom to explain his actions. Pete's first step to prepare for the meeting was to plan exactly what he wanted to discuss. (This is especially important when you're seriously committed to a project, task, or goal that will show your upper-management potential.)

To plan well, make an outline or agenda which lists what you want to say and how you want to say it. By having a written outline, you won't forget vital points because of tension and anxiety. You're also less likely to ramble, repeat yourself, or have pauses that make you appear unsure of yourself. In your preparation, provide the other party to the conflict with the pertinent information that will help him or her understand your action or decision.

For instance, Pete noted in his outline that he would begin by explaining that he had been part of the team that created and developed the architectural plans, so he knew that no further changes would be made. He would also note that he wanted to end the explanation with a statement such as, "I hope you now understand that I acted as I did because I felt any further delay would have been detrimental to both the client and us."

Of course, your outline will be thorough, but all you'll take with you to the meeting is an abbreviated version. This shortened guide will help you remember key points so you'll be able to speak in a poised, seemingly off-the-cuff manner, even though you will have rehearsed the important verbal responses out loud before the actual meeting.

When it's time for your meeting, be flexible with your verbal responses. The chances are good that you won't need everything you've prepared, but having a backlog of expressions is a mental savings account that will give you confidence.

Your abbreviated outline should be a single paper, with a word or phrase for each idea that can trigger what you want to say. Here's how Pete's abbreviated version keyed into these major points looked:

- *Positive premise:* "I'm always concerned about company protocol and rules, but this client needed the blueprints the next day."
- *Boss unavailable:* "I tried to see you, to get your okay after the client called, but you were tied up in meetings."
- *Blueprints overdue:* "We were already three days late in delivering the blueprints."
- *Continue to explain:*

  1. Client extremely upset, in angry phone call. Demanded plans sent by overnight express.

160

2. Plans were already finalized and approved by Tom in prior meetings.
3. Violated only the procedure of obtaining the official okay.
4. Tom always fulfilled this requirement in past.
5. Decided it was best for the department (directly relates to Tom, as team head) and best for the firm to comply with client's demands immediately.
6. Immediate result—client was pleased with both the fast action and the blueprints.

In the final analysis, Pete's well-prepared explanation was the forerunner to promotion as next team head. This satisfactory conclusion came about because Pete showed himself as a person who could speak with managerial skill and could make a responsible decision; thus he was plainly a candidate for the ranks of upper management.

CHAPTER 15

How to Convey or Cope With Bad News

"This is not something we wanted to have happen."

With our current cost-conscious climate and the subsequent decline in corporate loyalty, few managers are immune from the task of relaying bad news to others. In fact, this task often causes psychological strain, which is increased when managers giving the bad news identify with the recipients. When the managers have a strong feeling for others, they agonize over hurting their co-workers.

That was the position Jerry was in when, as a department head in a plant that manufactured plastic processing machinery, he had to tell Chuck, an assistant, that the job of senior mechanical designer, which Chuck had been hoping for, had been given to someone else.

Chuck had been with the plant six years; as soon as the opening was posted, he began to campaign hard for the job. After several conferences with top management, he expected the promotion. At the last moment, however, top management decided to hire a mechanical engineer from outside the plant. And Jerry, as Chuck's immediate boss, had to convey the news to Chuck.

When You Convey Bad News

Along with telling employees a promotion, raise, or bonus has been denied, other examples of bad news managers must relay include such things as austerity measures and budget cuts, cancelled contracts or projects, insufficient funds for hiring new employees, interdepartmental consolidations, transfers and relocations, and mergers or acquisitions.

How Can You Handle These Situations?

When you're the manager who must give the bad news, how can you maximize your verbal skills to convey what people don't want to hear? Here are four tips:

1. *Be straightforward.* Be honest with the other person and state the problem or explain the situation directly. "Straight talk involves honesty with yourself as well as with others," says Paula Kurman, director of Communicational Judo. "Know what it is you're thinking and feeling. Then be able to say it in a way which fits the context. You don't have to be brutal with honesty and use it as a club. Nonetheless, it's important to be able to talk straight."

Tony Cipollone, training director at Metroweb Corporation, agrees that managers should get right to the point:

Simply come out and say what has to be said. If a company's results are not what they should be, or if you're having some kind of operational difficulty, provide some background into what has happened. Make a connection between the bad news and how this news affects both the receiver and you as manager.

For example, your company's profitability has been low for the second half of the year, so, as an austerity measure, no annual bonuses will be given. You particularly hate to tell an employee who you know is counting on the bonus to remodel a room in his house. Instead of beating around the bush come right out and say, "Our profits are down and as a result no one is getting a bonus." Leading up to this bad news gradually won't make it easier to take.

2. *Act promptly.* Most management experts say you should act fast to give bad news. This was especially important for Sam, the second-floor manager in a large department store, when told by his boss that the fragrance department (which up until then had separate managers—Betty for women's goods and Joe for men's) was scheduled for consolidation, with one manager for both. Sam was instructed to tell Betty that Joe, who had been there longer, would manage the consolidated department and she would work under him.

"Relaying that news was difficult," explained Sam, "partly because the decision was made while Betty was vacationing in Florida. I knew she expected to move up eventually to a buyer's job, and since she was doing first-rate work, she had every reason to expect a promotion instead of a demotion.

"I agonized whether to speak to her the day she returned from vacation or to wait a day or two until she got settled in. But the news was out all over the store, and as her manager I knew it was essential to act on this bad news at once so that Betty would hear it from me rather than someone else."

Sam steeled himself to get to Betty immediately with, "How can I tell you, Betty? We have to cut back and consolidate two jobs—yours and Joe's—and since Joe has seniority he's going to manage the department and you will be under him. I'm sorry! I didn't expect this, and I'll do whatever I possibly can to help make this new arrangement work.''

3. *Prepare a script.* As for other situations, having a script ready will help you deal with difficult encounters. Naturally, you won't memorize the speeches or read them word for word. But having your words set out will help you get your head together and give order and sequence to your presentation of the news.

For example, the manager of a branch office of a nationwide temporary employment service received word from the main office that her branch would be closing at the end of the year. At that time the key people in the office would be transferred to another city.

"I knew it would be best to give the employees full information about the closing and relocation before anyone had a chance to come up with questions and reactions," the manager says, "so I set up what I wanted to say in a two-minute spiel and then called the people into my office." She explains how she began with, "I've called you together for some rather distressing news," and then without pulling any punches, she added, "This office is closing at the end of the year, and we're all being asked to relocate. It's certainly not something we wanted to happen. But this is the way it is."

"Most of the people were so taken aback it took time to digest the news," she recalls. "Because I explained it so fully, as a result of writing my script, it took several days before they came back with, 'What more can you tell us now?' By then I had another script for what I needed to say."

4. *Stand firm.* Don't back down once you've given out the bad news. For example, when the young publisher of a florist-industry trade magazine purchased a small landscaping journal, he inherited a journal contributor who'd been coasting along for several years with mediocre work.

"He thought he was set for life," says the publisher, "because, in his words, he 'had a deal' with the owner of the landscaping journal. But he was bad news all the way, and I didn't intend to keep him on board unless he upgraded his work.

I knew he was capable of doing good things, because he had once been tops, but through the years he'd completely sloughed off."

The publisher relayed the bad news via a letter, in which he made suggestions for improving the contributor's work. "He reacted by phone," the publisher explains, "with a 'How dare you?' attitude, followed by personal attacks on me and a series of ludicrous remarks like, 'Why are you so against me? Why are you nonsupportive? Why is it your place to criticize my work?' "

The publisher turned the remarks around with the response, "I am supportive, and it *is* my place to bring out the best in you—because if we can't move forward, we can't proceed together." The publisher recalls, "I spoke calmly, but firmly, and even though the guy expected I'd say, 'Okay, I goofed,' I kept my stance and didn't back down. In the end, after several phone calls, he agreed on a plan for getting his work back on track."

When You Hear Bad News

As a manager you are not exempt from being on the receiving end of bad news. Here are three common examples managers invariably pinpoint as bad news they don't want to hear.

1. *You're losing a valued employee.* When Janet, a real estate developer, learned she was losing the administrative assistant who kept her life in order, her impulse was to burst into tears—despite her strong convictions against women who cry in the workplace. "My first thought was, 'I'll never be able to function,' " she recalls. "But finally when I got my head together I realized there's no irreplaceable person. Somewhere there would be somebody else who could fill my needs."

Granted, it's always a setback to lose a valued employee.

But, instead of wasting time on regrets, managers who have been through this suggest concentrating on immediately finding a replacement and (instead of dwelling on the bad news and the employee you've lost) be glad for the fine service you gained in the years you employed him or her. You might say to your employee, "Naturally, I'm sorry to lose you, but I wish you the best in what you do next," or "Because you've done so well in this job, it would be helpful to me if, prior to your departure, you would prepare a policies and procedures handbook for your successor."

2. *You're being pulled off a job.* In *The Art of Getting Your Own Sweet Way,* Philip B. Crosby relates the story of Charlie Barry, an operations director of a Chicago manufacturing facility who was chosen to install, and become general manager of, a new plant in a southern city. If successful, the plant would serve as an example for other operations starting up in the South.

Charlie was elated to be tapped for the job, and until the new division was built, Charlie moved into a warehouse to begin production, train people, and get established.

Although he was never quite able to achieve either the output the company had expected or real acceptance in the new community, Charlie blamed the plant's temporary facilities and felt that things would be different when the personnel moved into the new plant. However, eight months after the move, Charlie was called back to Chicago as a "staff assistant," a spot traditionally held open for executives who failed.

Charlie couldn't understand why the board had pulled him from the job. But in analyzing the situation—and the bottom-line basics—Philip Crosby points out that from the first it was actually a communications problem. To begin with, Charlie and his boss both started out with different opinions concerning how to measure the total success of the project. Moreover, Charlie never understood the importance of community relations and involving the town in his venture. "If Charlie had had periodic meetings with top management to discuss his progress, his future planning, and the problems that existed, he would have become aware very soon that the board was interested in using this operation as a prototype for future expansion and vitally interested in community relationships," writes Crosby.[1]

If you experience a situation where you're pulled off a job, don't just brood in silence, "I don't understand." Instead, ask your manager or management team for an appointment to review what led up to your job switch. You can say: "It's important for me to understand where I fell short in handling the job in the way you wanted it done. I would appreciate it if you'd level with me so it won't happen again."

3. *You're facing a company takeover or restructuring.* The bad news that managers frequently hear has to do with mergers and organizational shifts. Every manager should know how to maximize his or her chances in these cases. But most executives agree that it's difficult to make hard and fast rules, since each situation is different. For example, is the change in status a friendly or a hostile merger? Is the company being taken over by an organization in a similar industry, or will it be part of a conglomerate?

"This will affect . . . whether you're going to keep your job and what it will be," says Don Christman, a consultant in the banking and financial industry.

> At this time, people have different instincts. Some hope the situation will come out all right in the end. Others go right to the boss's office and say, "Do I still have a job?" or "Where do I stand?" If you do this, and don't have a really good or rational basis for doing it at the particular time, it can reveal an awful lot of personal insecurity.

> It's a real tightrope, a matter of exercising good judgment and trying to create suitable situations where you can talk with your superiors and people in the company confidentially—or sometimes on a nonconfidential basis to get a fix on what's really going on.

Christman explains that the goal should be to create a situation whereby it seems to the people involved that speaking up about the change is an appropriate thing for you to do. Your communication should never be viewed as a panicky rushing around without any rational thought.

Phyllis Macklin, of the career management and outplacement firm Minsur, Macklin, Stein & Associates, suggests that a manager go to his or her boss and say, "I'm concerned and I know you are too, but you're one step closer to the truth than I am, so I'd appreciate it if we can have an understanding that, as you learn details, you will share them, until something actually happens." But, as Macklin points out,

It's almost impossible to get true information, and a manager needs to recognize that absolute truth will not be shared until the most senior person decides what the final outcome is going to be.

If the chairman of the board hasn't made a decision about how much he needs to reduce his staff, then there's no action till that time. But be forewarned when an acquiring company says "We're not terminating anyone," you need to add *today*, because anything can happen tomorrow.

Managers and executives continually emphasize that when the symptoms of a merger or restructuring appear, people need to start assessing themselves, their commitment and value to the company, their years of service, and other similar aspects of their career.

"People can speak up and ask the person ahead of them what he thinks their chances are," declares David Eyler, manager of an educational project. "But it's more effective if it's something that basically doesn't need to be asked.

Positioning yourself at the last minute is always a difficult thing. But if you make yourself valuable every day, you stand a better chance of coming out favorably.

When you constantly take the temperature of your situation throughout your working years, you have a feel for your standing and value—whether you're in a precarious position and are going to be lopped off as soon as someone figures out how to do it, or whether you've made yourself an essential player so that the people at the top will figure out how to retain you.

Whether you're the manager who conveys bad news or the one who must cope with it, always use your best verbal skills in an honest and straightforward way. When you give bad news, you can usually begin by saying, "I'm sorry to have to tell you that. . . ." And when you're on the receiving end, you can respond with such phrases as, "What can we do to fix this?" or "What will be the best action for everyone concerned?"

CHAPTER 16

Firings and Terminations

"Unfortunately, this is the end of our working relationship."

The bad news managers want to avoid most is telling another person his or her services are no longer needed. In fact, terminations are such an ordeal that many managers are quick to admit that they postpone these confrontations hoping, by some miracle, the situation will improve or the employee will quit.

Richard K. Irish, author of *Go Hire Yourself an Employer,* recalls, "I have a friend who had to fire a member of his law firm. The staff member was unproductive and unable to get along with others. But it took my friend three full years to actually fire the man. When it was finally done, it was so much better for everyone that he felt a tremendous load had been lifted from his shoulders."

Admittedly, having to fire someone puts a load on a manager's shoulders, and the strain is invariably heightened by the way today's companies must worry about potential legal costs if workers file compensation claims or bring suits against their employers. In addition, there is a certain amount of guilt in saying, "We must let you go." A manager feels responsible for people's egos as well as their loss of income. In some situations, managers believe that a person who fails is their failure, too. They think, "I shouldn't have hired him in the first place," or "If I had trained him properly, I would have seen what was going wrong and helped him."

Regardless of your emotions, if you keep a person who ought to be fired, you weaken the morale of other employees. Also, it's unfair to the people who must compensate for that person's problems. In the final analysis, all managers have to harden themselves to dismiss an employee when the reasons are right.

Jean Firstenberg, when she became director of the American Film Institute, found that one of her first responsibilities was to cut the staff. "When I came on board and was told that I was a hundred fifty thousand dollars over budget, I automatically thought of ways to raise money," she said. "I didn't want to think of the necessity for staff cutbacks, but I eventually learned that this was the wrong way to manage. I knew I had to steel myself to discharge people who were not absolutely essential to the operation."[1]

Sooner or later, most managers have to terminate employees, so it's important to learn how to do it; how to deliver the verbal message as humanely and effectively as possible. The following pointers will help you convey unwelcome news in a satisfactory way.

Before Termination

Performance appraisals are a good way to warn people that their work is of poor quality. But in addition to these formal appraisals, you need ways to give employees warnings before actually firing them.

Many companies have their own procedures that must be

followed for this. But if you have flexibility, management experts I've interviewed suggest a procedure in which, as a verbal first warning, you tell an employee what she or he is doing wrong. You might say, "We've trained you, and you've had every advantage. But you're still not performing up to our standards. I'm putting you on probation to see if you can overcome the problems you're having."

The second warning is a written one, followed by another meeting with the employee during which you can say, "Two months ago we agreed to meet at this time, so let's review the results of your effort. We'll go from beginning to end to see where you stand. Why don't you start first by giving me your impression?"

If a person's work continues to be unsatisfactory, you can continue to explore what's wrong, but simultaneously you should tell the employee that the job is hanging in the balance and that dismissal may result if things don't improve. This system of warnings is much fairer than silence or indirect signs of disapproval, followed by sudden dismissal.

As you progress along the warning system, document your warnings in writing, ideally in agreements signed by the employee and containing dates and descriptions of the infractions plus the dates of the warnings. This documentation shows a person's errors and limitations, and indicates how and when you made efforts to help. It also shows that you have showed no bias in regard to age, race, sex, and so forth. This record is your strongest protection if a dismissed employee decides to file a suit.

The Time and Place for Termination

If the end results of your warnings point to termination, use the only right way to fire: first-hand and face-to-face, at the appropriate time and place.

Naturally, the right time depends on the situation. There's

no perfect procedure, and managers disagree on what's the right time. Some believe the firing should never be conducted over lunch or on a Friday, holiday, anniversary, birthday, or other important event in a person's life.

"When a termination occurs between 4:30 and 5:30 on Friday, the person is left with an empty building and a family to face, a weekend at home to brew, and no one to talk to about the reality," explains Phyllis Macklin, a partner in the New Jersey-based career management and outplacement firm of Minsuk, Macklin, Stein & Associates.

> The best time is early in the week—Monday or Tuesday in the morning—so the person you fire has the availability of professional and corporate personnel for the questions and other matters he or she needs to discuss.
>
> As far as location—and whether it should happen in the person's office or the boss's—the most important thing is to do it in a spot where there is absolute privacy and where the fired person can compose himself.

The Dialogue

Most of the time there's a company policy for making dismissals. But as the person's manager, you will want to use an approach that enables the employee to keep his or her self-respect. For example, it's helpful to comment on some favorable aspects of the person's work. Unless the work is really bad (and the series of warnings document that), give the employee a reason for the firing that will keep his or her ego from being crushed.

"I have wrestled with the problem of whether to tell the whole truth or not for many years," reports Henry Rogers, "and I've finally concluded that for me it is better to tell a little white lie." He continues,

To tell someone that he or she is incompetent is rather cruel and insensitive, so I skirt the issue by creating an impersonal, if fictional situation. I say "We are restructuring the department," or "Economic conditions demand that—" or "We are taking the company in another direction." I just can't bring myself to say to another human being "You're lousy at your job. That's why I'm firing you." Maybe the person thinks he knows the truth but hopes he's wrong. With my little white lie, I've at least given him the opportunity to save face in a situation that is very uncomfortable for both of us.[2]

If you feel it is better to be more direct about the below-par performance, ask the employee to come to your office, then get to the point quickly. After telling him to sit down and make himself comfortable, Phyllis Macklin proposes saying, "As you know we've been reviewing your work and, as I've discussed with you before, everything has been written down and thought through. Unfortunately this is the end of our working relationship. Your last day will be Friday, March 21. You'll be paid till. . . ."

Once you give the termination notice and have provided advice on severance pay, offer other supports. This is a vital part of the firing interview. Macklin recommends offering the following, depending on the situation (in every case, however, unless you're the top person on the totem pole or the owner of your own firm, be armed with the full backing of the personnel department):

1. *Offer resignation.* Help the person save face and retain self-dignity by leaving open the option to resign. "For the option, you can talk about such things as 'by mutual agreement,' 'new opportunities,' 'other interests to pursue,' or any other reason the person selects," suggests Macklin.

2. *Determine the announcement.* Agree on how the termination is going to be announced. Employees at all levels can be helped with a face-saving announcement.

Macklin suggests you say, "We need to talk now about how you'd like to announce this." She adds, "For instance, when someone at the highest level of an organization is terminated, the company can arrange for a press release stating the person is resigning to write his memoirs, move on to something else, or whatever. This provides another way for the terminated person to maintain dignity.''

3. *Mention options.* Discuss outplacement or other benefits that may be available. For instance, corporations terminating employees often call in outplacement firms—specialists who help ousted employees in the job search. Advises Macklin,

> If outplacement is to be offered, say "You will be working with so-and-so, and you have an appointment with that person on. . . ." You may also tell the employee, "Louise in personnel will see you at. . . ." And if the person has had perks, you may be able to say, "Your membership will be allowed to continue to. . . ." Cutting off perks can mean a great deal in the loss of dignity and face.

4. *Structure a reference statement.* The exiting person will need job references for his or her next position. Say to the person, "Let's prepare a statement so that when you need to use the company as a reference, you'll have it."

Phyllis Macklin adds

> If the person asks you what you will say for reference, tell him exactly what you can honestly say that will either help him get a job or at least not interfere with his efforts, since a company can be sued for saying anything that prevents another person from employment.
>
> Depending on your reasons for firing, you may be able to tell him you'll be giving him a reference for a job at which he can probably do better, refer him to other companies, and direct him to acquaintances if you know they're doing some hiring.

Keep the interview short. Macklin specifies that a termination meeting should never last more than ten or fifteen minutes.

Throughout the meeting, stick to facts rather than feelings and make no reference to personal issues unrelated to work or to accusations from other employees unless they're involved in the issues. By all means, let the person have some say, because the more talking done the better. And as you make suggestions, remind the individual that this may be a chance to get a job with more of a future.

When everything has been addressed, ask the terminated employee to repeat his or her understanding of the termination. Make sure the individual has heard what you have said, and see that everything is documented in the file. "In some cases," says Macklin, "the person can come back for another interview after the initial shock has worn off."

Following the termination, consider the remaining person- nel and plan your approach so they understand the facts and are assured their jobs are intact—if the latter is the case. "They need to know they had no control over a person's firing and that the fired person's project will continue," concludes Macklin. "You can say, 'Art Smith is going to be assigned on a temporary basis' or 'So-and-so is being promoted.' "

Reactions to Termination

On occasion, a terminated person may exhibit almost a sense of relief, and say, "Okay, I understand, I expected it." Obviously, you can then respond with, "I appreciate your willingness to recognize this was going to happen."

But generally you can anticipate assorted reactions such as disbelief, hopelessness, helplessness, anger, hurt, disappoint- ment, and shocked silence. "The person who is shocked is not facing reality," states Macklin.

He's holding in all feelings, so the objective, as already mentioned, is to get the person to talk. Ask, "Do you understand what I am saying?" "How do you plan to tell your wife?" "What do you want me to tell your secretary?"

If a person will not speak and is really giving evidence of severe trauma, you may need to alert the human resources department to be available.

On the other hand, an angry person may speak out with crying, shouting, and cursing. That person may say, "What am I going to do now? I have kids in college," or "I'll never be able to get another job."

But, again, you must allow that person to talk. Respond with, "I can understand how you feel. You have worked hard for this company, and it's difficult to go through this situation. I can see why you're upset."

As you say these things, however, make sure your response is firm. Refrain from arguing and being defensive. And make it clear that the final decision has been made and that there will be no further appeal.

Security Situations

Although it is desirable to give people sufficient termination notice rather than shoving them out the door, there are occasions when for security reasons you must let them go with very little notice.

Phyllis Macklin tells the story of a 50-year-old executive who had been with the same corporation for most of his career. There was a cutback in the company and his job was phased out. But because he was involved in research and development, his boss—(after giving him outplacement information)—had to say to him, "For security reasons we will need you to hand in your badge and relinquish your key. I'll meet you in your office, and a security guard will be there to escort you and your belongings to the door."

Naturally, if an employee is fired because he is unstable or untrustworthy, the last thing you should do is let him remain on company premises, where he may be tempted to gain revenge by stealing, sabotaging equipment or records, or demoralizing other employees with accusations and falsehoods. For example, an editor for an encyclopedia company sought revenge for his dismissal by sabotaging the company's computer system and trying to rewrite history. Before he was caught, he had substituted the names of some of the company's employees for historical figures and Allah for Jesus in numerous passages of the encyclopedia.[3]

When You're the One Being Terminated

As pointed out in Chapter 11, all managers should schedule a performance review to ask, "How am I doing?" Simultaneously, they should document their status and what aspects of their work they need to correct to improve their job performance.

But if things don't work out even after the reviews and warnings, and you are to be terminated, listen carefully to what is said and be prepared to respond with questions. For example, Phyllis Macklin suggests the following, as they pertain to your situation:

1. What is the specific reason for the termination?
2. What date will I be leaving?
3. What are my termination benefits?
4. How long can I keep my club memberships?
5. Can I purchase the company car?
6. Will I be given outplacement service?
7. Will I be provided with office space while I seek new employment and, if so, for how long?
8. What will the company say when I need a reference? Will you put that statement in writing?
9. How long will I be paid?

10. What will be the relationship between my severance pay and the contribution I have made?

The amount of severance is important. "[It] is something that is often forgotten," explains Macklin. "But a person who has worked for a company for twenty years and made a major contribution deserves more than someone who has only worked for five.

Some companies have absolute policies based on level, salary, and period of employment. Others design severance per individual. But there's usually a pool of money for severance so managers should ask for it.

I know of a person who worked for a company for six weeks after leaving a significant job and secure work history and who got a new boss with a different set of goals. When she was terminated, she was offered two weeks' severance. But she asked for more and ultimately got six weeks.

In that case, as in others, there was money available. But often people have to ask for it, because obviously the person terminating an employee has a certain obligation not to give away the store.

Regardless of how you view the news of being fired, there's always a positive outlook: The people not appreciated in one corporation may be of real value in another.

Dr. Mortimer R. Feinberg, an industrial psychologist, sums this up:

Some years ago I brought some rough stones home from South America. I took them to Hans Stern, president of a large international jewelry company, and I still remember his answer when I asked if they had any worth.

"I'm interested in fine jewelry, and you can't make fine jewelry out of those raw stones," the jeweler replied. "But even though they're no good for me at this particular time in my organization, someone will be able to find a way of making something from them and doing well.''

So it is with people. The employee to whom you convey bad news may have potential in the next job. Or even if you receive the bad news yourself, remember you may be a winner somewhere else.

CHAPTER 17

Unwelcome Talk: Questions, Gossip, Rumors

"I don't believe in circulating information I wouldn't want written on my office wall."

Unless you're pursuing your management career in an ivory tower, chances are you'll be asked one or more of the following:

"Why aren't you married?"

"Did your father leave you some money?"

"How's your divorce going?"

"What do you pay for rent?"

"How much do you earn?"

"Does your wife (husband) make a good salary?"

"How high is your mortgage?"

"How expensive was that suit?"

Other favorite questions—such as, "How old are you?" "Do you plan to have children?" and "What are your religious beliefs?"—are illegal in job interviews. But once you're established in an organization, some colleagues think nothing of asking these unwelcome, quite personal questions. You can't be prepared for all of them. But you certainly should be armed with verbal responses to the major ones. You should also know how to handle company gossip and rumors.

Questions That Invade Your Privacy

When you're faced with an awkward question, find the motive behind the question and try to understand why the person is asking it. For example, is the person concerned, curious, confrontational, insensitive, or malicious?

Susan Hayes, president of Results Design Group, an Ohio-based organization that specializes in total quality management consulting, suggests asking why the person is asking the question:

Sometimes, especially between manager and employee, a boss will ask a question of a personal nature to establish and maintain a relationship, without realizing it might appear confrontational, striking a sensitive area.

For instance, at one time I was working with an upper-middle manager who was going through a divorce. One day his boss called him in and asked, right out of the blue, "How's your divorce going?" That was an uncomfortable question for the middle manager because he didn't want people at work talking about his personal situation.

When we discussed it, I suggested that at his next opportunity he speak to his boss privately, thank him for his interest, and say right up front, "Are you concerned about my ability to do my job because of my pressures at home? If so, I'd like to have a conversation with you."

When the middle manager tried Hayes's advice, he discovered that the boss had gone through a similar experience years before, and wanted to coach the manager on how to minimize having his personal situation interfere with his work life. The boss's question ultimately strengthened their relationship. In the future when problems came up (child custody, time off from work, or a request for less travel), the middle manager could negotiate his needs more effectively.

Personal Questions Relating to Work

Sometimes it's difficult to answer questions that straddle the line between personal and business matters, especially if you're anxious to postpone the answer. But if the question is business-related, you can't put off answering it forever. You need to offer a straightforward reply, or a strategy that will buy you more time, if the situation warrants that.

In one such case, a middle manager had been offered a transfer to a better job in another city. His wife was opposed to moving, however, since she had a business in the town where they lived. The manager was in a quandary, so when his supervisor asked, "Has your wife agreed to the transfer?" the manager responded, "I'm still working on it. Just give me a little bit longer."

By the expression on the boss's face, however, the manager knew this was a case where a personal inquiry was also a legitimate business question. Sensing this, he immediately added in a straightforward manner, "Just give me tonight, and I promise you I'll have an answer tomorrow." That night he confronted his wife with the issue, and after hours of discussion the couple came up with this arrangement: He would accept the transfer, she would stay put and continue her business, and they'd have a "commuting marriage" in which they'd spend their weekends together. The next day the manager told his boss, "I've decided to take the transfer."

In another situation, a young manager was three months pregnant but unwilling to announce her pregnancy and arrange

184

for maternity leave. She took time off for her doctor's appointments and covered up her fatigue at work. But when her boss asked, "Are you by any chance pregnant?" her strategy was to rely on her reputation for having a sense of humor; she answered lightheartedly with a disarming smile, "Do I look like I'm having quintuplets? I'd like to be the first to know."

Since her pregnancy wasn't affecting her work, her strategy of using humor alleviated the need to be straightforward until she was ready—two months later—to announce her pregnancy. At that time she went to her boss and said, "I know you've already guessed it. But now I'm ready for the world to know I'm having a baby in August. I'd like maternity leave from August until January 1."

Questions Unrelated to Work

When questions of a strictly curious nature come along, simply refuse to deal with them by answering in a straightforward or flippant way, but without employing a how-dare-you-ask? attitude.

Certainly one of the most popular nonbusiness questions is the inevitable "How old are you?" Young or old, we're all curious about other people's ages. But you don't have to answer these inquiries at all if you don't believe in numbers. Instead you can respond:

"I'm sorry, that's one question I never answer."

"I prefer not to say."

"I'm sure we'd both prefer to avoid personal questions."

Whether or not you make an issue of divulging your age, it may appear that you are on the defensive, afraid of what others will think of your true age. You can counter that with a smile and a flippant, ridiculous answer:

"Today I feel like a babe in arms."

"Today I feel a hundred years old."

When you don't come up with a number, people may persist with indirect questions like, "When did you graduate from college?" "What year did you get married?" and "When were your children born?" A flippant answer to these is, "In this century."

Although no one can ask you about your religious beliefs during a job interview, the question "Do you go to church?" is often asked later on. It's a query that seems to be aimed at assessing your integrity. Susan Hayes suggests that perhaps the persistent threat of mergers makes some managers want to check people's integrity. "It's a way of finding out more about people and their ethics."

Whatever its intention, this is a more subtle question than "What are your religious beliefs?" But it doesn't require an answer. If you prefer not to deal with it, simply respond with, "That's really not part of this business" or "I believe that's a personal matter and not relevant here."

Answer a Question With a Question

When you don't want to answer a personal question when it's asked, turn the question back to the person who asked it in the first place. Then it doesn't seem as if you're evading the issue, yet you refrain from giving away personal matters. And this can be done for difficult business situations as well as uncomfortable personal ones.

Susan Hayes explains:

For example, a manager was involved in a meeting with a very important supplier. The purpose of the meeting was to work out a conflict.

In the course of the confrontation, the supplier asked

186

the manager, "Where do you stand on handling this?" The manager's smart response was, "What would you think the most valuable way to handle it would be? What issues do you think we should be talking about?"

Gossip and Rumors

Every company has its share of light, harmless gossip: the who's-doing-what-when-and-where that even the most virtuous among us indulge in from time to time. But unfortunately most organizations also have in-house villains—the manipulators, backbiters, and malicious competitors who whisper behind people's backs or try to hurt others with uncalled-for quips.

These people injure others by attempting to show, through implication, the negative aspects. Their words and actions are underhanded and under cover. They wreak their havoc by cutting productivity, provoking turmoil, frustrating and demoralizing people, and causing anger, tension, embarrassment, and stress.

There are various reasons why rumormongers exist, but, according to psychologists and management consultants, in business the primary reasons are:

1. They want to have power, but they're vulnerable and insecure. They believe they have little power and control over their own lives.
2. They feel that the world is threatening and that most people can't be trusted.
3. They sense a lack of recognition for their own work. Since they can't deal with this frustration, they hit below the belt.
4. They have a chronic case of jealousy and think that someone else is making more money and doing better than they are.
5. They want to get back at others for something.
6. They don't want anyone else to interfere with their goals.

187

7. They mistakenly believe that undermining others will give them more credibility.

Recognizing the motivation powering these people can help you deal with their actions. As always, strong verbal skills are your best arms.

When You're the Victim

If you're the victim of gossip, you have to develop a plan to remove the trouble as quickly as you can. First, try to find out the motive behind the gossip. Then encourage the gossips to openly express their thoughts and feelings. By doing this, sometimes you can dismantle the screen, determine the real problem, then clear the air and get matters resolved.

"It's always important to address gossip head on, because letting it go is bad for you as a manager," states Hayes. "People get the idea you don't handle difficulty well."

Never let indirect attacks pass by without commenting on them. Address the problem in private by confronting the people who are spreading the rumors. Ask them, "Do you really mean what I hear you're saying?" "I gather you don't agree with me," or "Why don't we talk about what you meant?" The rumormongers may back away from your directness, but you make it clear that you see through them.

"One thing you can do is take someone who is undermining you out to lunch," suggests Hayes. "It can be a private meeting or you can invite a neutral person so you'll have three people. If the situation is really bad, and this meeting doesn't work, you can go to the person's boss and say, 'This is what I perceive is happening. I would like to have a meeting'—though ideally you'd like to resolve the problem, so the latter won't have to happen."

Marilyn Moats Kennedy, founder of an Illinois-based management consulting firm and author of *Office Warfare: Strategies for Getting Ahead in the Aggressive 80's,* insists you speak up. "You say to that person, 'I understand that you have been saying thus-and-so.' That person is going to say, 'Oh, no' or 'Who me?' or 'How could that be?' The response is, 'Good, I'm glad you didn't say it. That means I won't hear that on the grapevine anymore."

Another strategy to deflate rumors is to get one person to hear your side and then branch out to others until the rumor is laid to rest.

When You're Not the Victim

If you pass along gossip, you become associated with it. Unless it's directed toward you, it's better to set an example by not indulging in the gossip yourself. Don't give in to attempts to draw you into it. Along with being unprofessional, gossiping makes your colleagues wonder what you think or say about them.

As for rumors, simply don't repeat them. Refute them if you possibly can, or let them die in your office with, "I've heard that, too, but it's just a rumor. I know that it's not true."

Your Position as a Manager

Rumors eventually lead to employee unrest and lower productivity, so they are a major concern of management. Dr. Morris Spier, director of the industrial and organizational psychology programs at United States International University in San Diego, suggests that managers take a stand against gossip that destroys the reputation of other workers.

"While you can't stop all gossip—and would not want to stop all types because it's one way managers can find out about the problems that need to be solved," he adds, "you can set an example by not passing on gossip yourself and by announcing to your employees that spreading rumors about others is a good way to find yourself out of a job."

Susan Hayes makes a connection between gossip and performance appraisal. "Managers can let people know in [their] performance appraisals that they will be evaluated on how well they work and promote other people in the organization. If people know they're going to be evaluated on this, they tend to watch out for the undermining."

According to Hayes, "I coach a lot of teams, and team interaction is a fertile ground for rumor and gossip."

In one situation, I worked with a team in which three team members had worked together for a period of time before two new members were put on the team. When the new members were added, conflicts between the two forces developed and rumors developed about one of the new members.

The rumor was that the new member had gone behind the team's back and done things. To resolve the problem, I suggested to the new member that he bring the matter up at a meeting of the team by talking about such things as the relationship between the team and the supervisor.

The new team member shared his belief that it would be damaging to anyone on the team to spread gossip. "Not that I'm accusing anyone," he said. "But if gossip, rumors, and lies get out to our supervisor, we'll all be vulnerable."

As a result of his speaking up the team members made a mutual agreement to adopt a closed-book approach, so that whatever went on in their team work would not be shared with anyone else.

CHAPTER 18

Company Politics: The Who-Gets-What Game

"Let me think about that for a moment."

The business of company politics is everybody's business, since everyone in an organization plays the corporate who-gets-what game.

"Basically, office politics is the way the power pie gets divided," explains Marilyn Moats Kennedy, the founder of an Illinois-based consulting firm. "It's a complex game and a fact of life that can work either for or against you."

In her book *Office Politics*, Kennedy points out that playing politics can mean either steering clear of backbiting gossip or gleaning important information from the company grapevine. It can mean learning to be a dependable team player or finding a more experienced worker to show you the ropes. It can mean advertising your own potential for advancing on the job without becoming a pariah among your colleagues.[1]

Regardless of the objectives, however, company politics is

a game that requires a high verbal IQ. To win the game, you need the verbal agility that is discussed in this chapter.

The Games That Are Played

Kennedy stresses that anyone can use any part of the office politics structure to hurt or help somebody else. She also points out that office politics do not have to be a war game between "good" and "bad."[2] Most managers are in a position to be hurt and helped—as they and their colleagues compete for raises, promotions, transfers, and other important objectives.

How can you avoid being left behind on the political trail? How can you protect your turf when the maneuvering gets underway? The answer is to be aware of the common political maneuvers that contribute negatively to office politics. Learn to recognize the nasty games that are played:

1. The players make sure you don't get certain information you require for a particular job, and they slow you up with, "I'll get back to you." They never follow through with the approval you need.
2. The players set you up for failure by taking papers from your desk or losing assignments or memos you should have. Thus, you're delayed in getting your work done.
3. The players take credit for or claim rewards that you deserve. If they hear you're in line for a promotion, they hint to upper management that you might not be able to handle it, by saying, "Do you really think he can do the job?" or "Is she ready for a promotion?"
4. The players try to undermine, discredit, and negate your achievements.
5. The players hear of an idea you're working on and find a subtle way to present it to top management first. They act as though they initiated it, and you are an "also ran."

192

What to Say and Do

Take a firm stance when you are a victim of office politics. These five guidelines will help you maintain your position or turn the situation around.

1. *Assemble evidence.* If you're ever set up for failure—say, someone "loses" the assignment or memo that you should be getting or holds back on supplying information or a go-ahead—keep a log documenting your work activity, including the time you receive the work assignments, your memos, and information and go-aheads that don't come through. When you have established a pattern, take your findings to upper management.

2. *Confront the troublemaker.* If someone takes papers from your desk so you will be delayed and can't perform at your best, Kennedy suggests confronting that person with, "Of course, you didn't do it, but listen to what has been happening." Either that person will finger the one who did it or simply stand there silently. If he or she is silent, you can add, "The papers will never disappear again, will they?"

3. *Document your achievements.* Documentation is essential when someone is trying to undermine, discredit, or negate your achievements. Make sure what you have done is recorded both verbally and in writing. For instance, if you've increased sales by 15 percent, let the people in power know what you've done. Say, "Last year I brought in x dollars." Facts are facts, and when you have documentation your achievements can't be negated.

4. *Publicize your goals.* Since all managers run into people who try to claim undeserved credit, you can avoid problems by putting your plans on record with management. "I know a lot of managers who in their hearts want to empower their staff to achieve things," says Susan Hayes, the president of an Ohio-based total quality management consulting firm, "but at the same time there's the real fear they may be dealing with a staff member who may upstage them."

When managers are in that position, the solution is to make their goals clear to their upper managers right from the beginning. They should say, "This is what I'm going to produce. This is how I plan to do it. It may not always appear that I am the one who is personally going to achieve this, but these are the specifics on how I'm going to execute it."

It's to your credit as a manager to have the people who work for you perform well, but at the same time, make sure your goal and specifics are in writing. Then no matter how much someone wants to take credit or claim rewards that you deserve, you have established ahead of time what your goals for the project are and how you as manager are going to achieve them.

If, despite your best efforts, someone claims credit for something you've accomplished, Mark Clemente, a marketing director, suggests that you announce to that person, "I know what you did and my perception of you has certainly been colored by it. This may be an isolated incident, but you can bet that in the future I'm going to conduct myself and my dealings with you quite differently."

Says Clemente, "This doesn't have to be a yelling and screaming match, but you have to make it clear that you know the game the person is playing and you don't approve of it."

5. *Know whom you can trust.* Don't talk widely about your plans and ideas so that other people can pull them out from under you. Be as friendly and cooperative as you wish, but don't discuss your hopes for an upcoming job opening or promotion and don't publicize your bright ideas. There are people in every organization who are not creative themselves, but who manage to get ahead by taking other people's ideas and packaging them as though they were their own.

"If you have any degree of interpersonal savvy, after you've been burned a couple of times you're good at sizing those people up," states Mark Clemente.

Your bouncing off ideas with them should be predicated on their reputations and the experiences you've had with them.

There are people you can't trust because you've seen how they act. But, fortunately, on the other side of the coin, there are persons who are real straight-shooters. They won't take ideas and run with them, so I have no concern whatsoever saying, "I've got a great idea and I want to bounce it off of you."

How Involved Should You Be in Company Politics?

As I say at the start of this chapter, the corporate political arena is everybody's business. It's likely you'll become involved when you're the victim of political games, but is it possible otherwise to stay aloof of politics?

Many management consultants believe that it's possible to be an uncommitted observer. For instance, Susan Hayes feels a manager can stay out of the arena: "Suppose someone says to you, 'We want to know where you stand.' A good response if you want to remain uncommitted is to say, 'I don't know where I stand. I haven't had time to assess all the information. When I take a closer look at the issue I will have a better perspective.' "

Hayes explains that if this is said with the right tone and with the commitment to get back with a response, it's a satisfactory answer. "But you have to think before you act, and you also have to do what you personally believe in," she adds. "Managers are really looked down upon if they appear to sway with every political struggle, since this indicates they are opportunists who, in order to advance themselves, will go with whatever action they think is the most advantageous for them."

Before joining a political struggle in which you're not involved, you should assess the risk you'll be taking. "Unless you're willing to risk a lot in the struggle, it's best not to be very vocal," advises Hayes. "Sometimes if you're not immediately involved, the best way to react is not to react."

195

Hayes stresses that managers should follow what they think personally is the right thing to do. "I haven't seen people get a lot of value out of being involved in a political struggle. You never know who is going to be your next boss or peer." She cites the example of a young manager in a manufacturing facility. When she thought she was going to be transferred, the manager implicated herself in a political struggle that involved three other managers. "She was very vocal about one of them. Later, when her transfer didn't come through, she ended up working for the manager she'd been so vocal about."

Wherever you work, you'll meet rivalry and political maneuvering. Try to dispel the negatives with discretion and diplomacy. And although I stress documenting your achievements, when office politics is involved, don't *ever* criticize anyone in writing. Your words could come back to haunt you, as they did Bryant Gumbel, the co-host of the *Today* show, who wrote critically of his co-workers, only to have his memo discovered and relayed from New York to California.

PART IV

The Final Word

CHAPTER 19

Keep Up the Good Word

"Good morning! How are you today?"

Throughout this book I show how well-handled verbal responses can increase your visibility and enhance your management career. The experiences of many managers have demonstrated how verbal fluency, voice control, well-chosen words, and good listening skills provide the winning combination for achieving a managerial advantage. These verbal techniques will help you:

- Get the information you need.
- Make and respond to business requests.
- Showcase your ability at presentations and meetings.
- Conduct yourself on the telephone.
- Train your personnel.
- Give and receive effective performance appraisals.
- Offer and respond to criticism.
- Resolve conflicts and avoid confrontations.
- Convey and cope with bad news, including firings and terminations.

- Handle unwelcome talk.
- Deal with company politics.

It's equally important, however, to keep up the good word in your other business encounters, both large and small, as you advance your career. In this chapter, some other situations are covered.

Be Prepared for Unexpected Encounters

Sometimes you know ahead of time that you will be facing a critical situation—say, being seated next to a VIP at a company banquet. But there are chance occasions when you may run into this same individual, perhaps standing on a train platform or getting a can of soda from the machine. The encounter is a good opportunity to make an impression on someone who might help you move ahead— *if* you're aware of his or her interests and *if* you're able to show off your verbal IQ.

"Your conversation must be interesting," writes Henry C. Rogers, the public relations guru. "You need important things to say, important subjects to discuss, and important observations to make."[1]

Marc Dorio, vice-president of a management consulting firm, tells the story of a young director of sales who, while flying to a meeting in a corporate jet, found herself sitting with three key executives. Because of the way she was able to talk about matters that interested the executives, she was viewed positively. Later, the word was passed to her boss that she was someone to watch.

Take Advantage of Informal Encounters

Informal meetings happen everywhere every hour of the day—in hallways, elevators, company cafeterias, and the like. They are part of every kind of social and professional event.

Marc Dorio offers an example of this: "When I was first in the management consulting business I stepped into the elevator one day and found myself alone with the chairman of the board of one of our clients. We had a 45-second ride together, but this was an opportunity. I knew from what I'd heard that his passion was golf."

With golf as his kick-off point, Dorio asked, "How's your golf game these days, Mr. ——?" The chairman of the board responded, "It's quite wonderful." Dorio continues, "He became so engrossed in talking about golf, that we walked out of the building together still speaking about it. Then out on the street we continued the conversation as we walked two blocks together. From then on, we'd always have a conversation whenever I met him in the halls while doing work for his company."

Phyllis Gillis, president of Entrepreneurial Communications, a public relations firm, confirms this. "Some of the best conversations I've had have taken place in halls, elevators, over lunch, at cocktail parties, in kitchens, and while waiting at a car wash with an executive of a large company."

Managers say hallways are a made-to-order spot for informal contacts with supervisors and co-workers. "I would never use hallways for presenting new ideas or going into a deep discussion about ideas already on the fire," explains a systems expert for a national data processing firm.

But I've found the best time to make contact with the real biggies in this company is in the hall. Often their doors are closed when you need to talk to them, and in some cases there's a company policy that you don't try to get in to speak to them when the door is shut.

When you see them walking down the hall, however, you can say, "I have a quick question for you" or "I need a clarification of your latest memo." Then, as you talk, pass the time of day so they'll get to know you better.

Even when you have no questions or business to conduct, Milo Sobel, a management educator, suggests that when you walk down a hallway, you make eye contact with people walking in the other direction. Say, "Good morning. How are you today?"

"It seems so obvious, but people don't do it," Sobel adds. "Maybe they're afraid of being thought of as weirdos. But once one person does that others pick up on it." Sobel continues:

> I personally would do that to all co-workers I pass. Then, assuming I pass them more than once and they begin to look familiar to me, I would take the initiative of introducing myself by saying, "Excuse me, I keep passing you, and it's rude of me not to introduce myself."
>
> You can say, for example, "My name is ——, and I'm in Accounting, down the hall. May I ask your name?"
>
> After people give you their name and tell you something about themselves, try to show interest with, "That sounds like an interesting job" (if, in fact, it is) or "That sounds fascinating [or terrific]." Add "If I can be of any help to you just remember my name is ——, and I'm down the hall."

Coffee breaks and other pauses in the day provide still other opportunities to interact with co-workers. "Few managers realize the significance social interaction plays in the work day," states Dr. Morris Spier, director of the industrial and organizational psychology programs at United States International University in San Diego.

"The informal communication system is the most effective way to disseminate noncontroversial information," he continues. "Good managers also learn to read the attitudes they pick up from employees during their break times together to find problems in the company that need correcting."

To get the most mileage from your breaks, take them with a variety of persons rather than the same people all the time. Also, note when and where your company's top people take their coffee breaks, and then head there for your coffee at the same time. Similarly, note where these people relax when they're not at their desks, and take your cues from that.

In some cases, you can set up an informal encounter without waiting for chance. For example, if your boss is a morning person, arrive early and speak with him before others come in. If you're a commuter, note which executives ride to work together and consider hitching rides occasionally with different groups.

Break Bread Together

In *Rogers' Rules for Businesswomen,* Henry C. Rogers quotes a woman in banking who said, "I make it a point to have lunch with someone from the bank two or three times a week. I never sit back and wait for an invitation. I invite key colleagues and in return there are times now and then when they invite me."[2]

When people dine together it tends to deepen relationships, since all of us like to do business with people we like. Consequently, make business breakfasts, lunches, and dinners (and even company-cafeteria meals) a time to mix business and pleasure, especially with well- informed co-workers.

Corporate training director Tony Cipollone advises, "It's a good idea to lunch with different people from different parts of the organization. In this way you can share information and find out what is going on in other parts of the business."

Stay alert for background information that seldom comes through formal channels. The knowledge you gain can be a great help in doing your own job. Plus, according to Cipollone, the information can dovetail:

For instance, even if you're not involved in higher-level meetings, where managers from different departments get together and talk about company-wide issues, you can at least put some things together from your shared information at lunch.

As a result, you can go to your boss and say, "I was talking to ———, and he said. . . . That seems to tie in with. . . . Can you tell me more about it, because it seems to me that here's an area that looks as though it would be worth doing something with?"

To present yourself at your best during a business meal, keep the following in mind:

1. Be comfortable to be with and easy to talk to by being at ease yourself. A little small talk establishing some common ground will get things off to a good start.
2. Once the ball is rolling, let other people talk. Ask questions and add to what they say.
3. If dining with people who are important to your advancement, take your cues from them. If they don't want to talk about business, and prefer to discuss sports or what's going on in world politics, go with that. Follow up later with, "I really enjoyed the other evening, and I've just been wondering about something I want to ask you." Only then bring up the business question.
4. Avoid questionable humor and stick to mainstream, non-offensive topics.
5. Mind your manners and practice etiquette.
6. Watch your drinking.
7. Don't order barbecued ribs!

Keep People Aware of Your Presence

As stated earlier, chances to speak up about yourself pop up nearly everywhere. Other good spots for presenting a good verbal image are meetings of service and social clubs or trade and professional associations, trade shows, conferences and conventions, and community and charity events. The previously mentioned woman in banking said, ''I know that being visible and making my peers and people in top management well aware of my presence is important to my future. I attend each of the occasional bank receptions and make certain that all the right people are aware of my presence.''[3]

Fortunately, there are ways to make people aware of your presence without appearing to boast. For example, Paula Kurman, of Communicational Judo, was at a dinner where the strangers she was sitting with seemed intellectual and they downplayed their image by the way they dressed. On the other hand, Kurman was dressed ''middle- of-the-road.'' The earrings she wore glittered, however, and she could sense almost at once that two of the people at her table had labeled her as frivolous. She explains what happened:

> We were all devoted to a serious cause, so I wondered how I could get them to understand that I really did have a brain between those earrings and that they had perhaps misjudged me.
>
> Naturally, I couldn't approach them with, ''Hello, I'm really an intellectual with quite a bit of schooling, and I'm interested in these issues, too.'' Instead, I let some time go by and entered the conversation very slowly. Finally, when the talk turned to a radio station's listenership, I made an informed comment. That seemed to make me okay and there was a definite shift in the way they looked at me.

As Kurman stresses, ''You *can* slip in words about yourself without carrying a sign printed 'Look who I am' or 'Look at what I do.' By every standard, the look-who-I-am brand of bragging—without good humor and grace—can be an embarrassing glimpse into a weak ego. But there's nothing wrong with a healthy self-interest, as long as you lay it on the table *gracefully*. Generally, if you're interested in someone else, that will spark an interest in you.''

Doe Lang, of Charismedia Services, also believes you can

talk about yourself without sounding like a braggart. "I will never forget talking to Dr. Vartan Gregorian, the well-regarded former president of the New York Public Library.

"He has tremendous communication skills and a great sense of wonder. And I'll always remember the way he said, as he looked back at his life, 'Little did I realize when I was a penniless Armenian immigrant that I would one day be head of the New York Public Library.' That one sentence covered his entire career," says Lang, "and it didn't sound like boasting. It sounded like wonder and excitement."

Doe Lang says that *anyone* can use this technique of matching the end to the beginning. Modify to your own situation that one phrase, "Little did I realize when I was a struggling stockboy [or whatever] that someday I would be. . . ." "When you say it with pleasure and delight, it does not come across as 'I'm wonderful.' "

In the final analysis, a good verbal IQ will strengthen your visibility and showcase your management potential. As everyone knows, the good guys are not always the winners and the race isn't always to the swiftest. And because you're human (and involved with other humans), everything won't always be perfect in the management world.

You have to expect some situations when even the finest verbal IQ won't achieve the results you want. But after learning what you can from these experiences, put them aside and move on to the other times, when your well-handled verbal communications turn your management career onto an upwardly mobile route. Through your solid verbal skills you can be as satisfied and successful as you want to be.

CHAPTER 20

Quick-Response Guide: More Than 300 Phrases to Use When You Are Put on the Spot

"Good words are worth much, and cost little."

—George Herbert

I've assembled here the many words and phrases that demonstrate a manager's ability to think, evaluate, and explain with a high verbal IQ. Many of these phrases have already been given in preceding chapters, but I've also added others. This Quick-Response Guide is a quick-and-easy reference for managers on the way up.

Adapt these expressions to your own personality—and your own situations—so you'll never come across as someone with a one-phrase-fits-all approach.

Highlighting Your Achievements

Last year I brought x dollars into this company.

I'm a hands-on person.

Here is the job that was done and here are the results.

The problem was, . . . and here's how we solved it.

I'm sure you'll be interested in the end results of. . . .

I hope you will agree with our feelings that this was a comprehensive effort that netted excellent results.

I was so pleased that I thought of . . . and was able to do. . . .

I was so delighted that, in spite of all the difficulties we had with shipping the product, I was able to come up with a new plan that will effectively obviate any such difficulties in the future.

You didn't ask for this, but in the course of my work this information surfaced.

Little did I realize when I was a struggling stockboy [or whatever] that someday I would be. . . .

Expressing Empathy and Interest

I understand how you feel about it, and I know that. . . .

I hope you will understand. . . .

I understand how strongly you feel.

It would seem that you. . . .

I can see that this matter is very important.

I understand your situation.

Your response is appropriate.

I see.

Here's what I'm hearing you say.

How's your project going?

Tell me what you're doing.

I really enjoyed the other evening, and I've just been wondering about something. I'd like your opinion.

Conveying a Sense of Urgency

I'll do it immediately.

I'll get right on it.

I'll go through a wall to do this.

I'll have it for you today.

Consider it done.

Don't worry—I'll take care of it.

Don't worry—it's taken care of.

It's being taken care of as we speak.

I'll take care of getting the answer.

We are working on it.

Cooperating and Compromising

Is there any way I can help out?

What can I do for you today?

We're in this together.

This is our mutual goal.

I'd appreciate your support for this project, and would welcome the opportunity to reciprocate.

Given what we know now, I don't think we ought to go in that direction. Let's compromise and move in this direction.

If you have a problem, come see me and we'll work on it together.

Please keep track of when the problem occurs and get back to me.

It's in our common interest to. . . .

Considering our mutual concern. . . .

Because of the value of our group effort. . . .

Complimenting and Reaching Out to People

You did a great job on that project.

You deserve a compliment for the way you handled that.

210

Good thinking on your part.

That was great work.

I'm glad my suggestion helped you out.

Here's an article I clipped that relates to. . . .

In my reading I've noticed how this trend shows the directions some companies are taking.

Excuse me—I keep passing you in the hall, and it's rude of me not to introduce myself.

My name is . . . and I'm in . . . down the hall. May I ask your name?

If I can be of any help to you, remember my name is, . . . and I'm down the hall.

Coping With Things That Go Wrong

Is this a legitimate complaint? If so, what can we do about it?

How can we make this better?

What can I do now?

How can we fix this situation?

If this is wrong, I'm going to come back to you with something that is right.

I know you're upset. Let's talk things over later.

I'd like a chance to work this out with you.

We know what the problem is. Let's focus on the solution.

Regardless of who's at fault, there's a problem here that has to be remedied immediately. Let's look at what we can do to remedy it.

There are still things we can try.

Give me a chance to come back to you with another solution.

Let's try. It might work.

This is nothing to fight over.

With all due respect, this is what the situation was.

What is the next step to make this better?

We have options. Here are some alternatives worth trying.

Defending Your Decisions and Actions

I felt that acting swiftly was the best decision for the company.

It was my intention to be responsible and efficient.

I would like to explain why this was done and how it helped the company. May I see you in your office this afternoon?

Here is the way I thought it should be done, and here is my reason for doing it.

Here's what I did. Here's why I did it. This was my thinking.

Here's what I was assigned to do, and here's what I did.

It was my impression that. . . .

It was my feeling that. . . .

It appeared to me you meant. . . .

Let me explain why I thought it was urgent. . . .

When I explain why I made that decision, you just might agree with me.

It's possible when you hear the facts that you might agree with my decision.

This was our purpose for doing it this way.

This is why I made those changes.

Frankly, I'm not at my best when someone attacks me.

Resolving Problems

What would you think the most valuable way to handle this would be?

What issues do you think we should be talking about?

What do you think a fair solution would be?

We have to do some talking about this. When is a good time for you?

Let's talk this over so we can. . . .

It just might be possible to manage that. . . .

Where do you think we should go from here?

Perhaps we can find a solution that will satisfy both of us.

I gather you don't agree with me. Would you like to talk about it?

I think we need a lot more information about. . . .

I haven't had time to assess all the information. When I look back at the issue, I will have a better perspective.

Let's wait till we both get all the facts before we try to settle this.

I'm sure we can discuss this to our mutual satisfaction much more productively when the shouting is over and we have some uninterrupted time.

There's something we need to talk about.

I have a problem I'd like to discuss with you.

What is it that's behind your objection?

Why do you as an individual seem to be so opposed to this?

I don't understand how your objection holds water.

Why won't this plan work?

I'd like a little better explanation or further discussion on why you think this isn't going to work.

I don't agree that this is anything that's standing in the way.

There's something else that's troubling you, and I wonder if you could try to get to that.

You seem to be dismissing this very simply.

Making Business Requests

Please make sure to work on this agenda today. As you can see, it's to go to . . . regarding the conference that's scheduled for next month.

Do you have any questions?

Do you have any suggestions?

What suggestions for implementation do you have?

I'll always have an open-door policy and be committed to you and your interests whenever you need to air them.

Responding to Business Requests

I'll do what it takes.

How would you like me to handle this?

214

I'm not completely clear about every aspect to which you may be referring, but I'll obtain full information for you.

I'm not quite sure of the meaning of some of your terminology.

I don't know, but I'll find out.

It will be important for you to give me clear guidelines about what you would like me to do, how you would like me to do it, and when you would like me to do it.

I have a quick question for you.

I need a clarification of your latest memo.

Can you help me out a bit by elaborating on that further?

It's probably not wise for me to try to handle this increased work load. I'm already a little overwhelmed with what I'm doing now. You may prefer to assign that task to someone else.

Maybe I shouldn't handle this new project this week because I'm already doing A, B, C, D, and E. Perhaps it would be in everyone's best interest if someone else takes on F, since I won't be able to give it the fair and thorough attention that I should.

I'd like to deal with this in the future and would be more than happy to talk to you about it then.

This priority must have my attention now.

I'm not sure that I can take it on at this moment.

Asking Questions

Did I understand you to say? . . .

If I understand you correctly, you said. . . .

Is that right?

Do you think we could agree to? . . .

What would you have liked me to say that I didn't say?

Why didn't you like what I said?

Would it be a good idea to consider? . . .

What alternates would you suggest?

Are you comfortable doing it this way rather than that way?

Do you see how this procedure can work?

Do you agree?

Do you think A is better than B?

Training Personnel

I just thought I'd touch base with you. I know you were doing well yesterday, but I thought you might have some questions or comments that will help you get more out of this training. Anything else we can discuss?

Do you think it might have been more effective if you had done? . . .

How do you feel about that?

Exactly why do you feel that way?

I'm always accessible.

I want you to feel I'm on your side.

I want you to succeed, and I'll do all I can to help you.

What can I do to help?

216

Meetings and Presentations

There will be a meeting, and this is why we're calling it.

I have some ideas and strategies to share with you.

I promise your time will be well spent.

We're here to discuss our proposed price increases and the methods we'll use to tell our customers about it.

The purpose of this meeting is to talk about our expansion program.

What do we in management need to do? How can we do it?

Let's keep that for later. This is the issue right now.

I think this is a concern of yours, too. What do you think?

We don't have a lot of time. We still have to deal with. . . .

We're getting together to review our performance for the last three months. Does anyone see any trends?

That's an interesting point. Perhaps we can discuss it at another time, but I don't think with the information that we have to present now that that is part of this discussion.

I wonder if you could explain further what information you'd like to obtain from that question. What are you looking for?

One question that's always asked about this is. . . .

Right before I began my presentation I was asked if. . . .

That is something I've been thinking about—how do you feel about it?

Are you telling me this is what you're thinking?

217

Giving Performance Appraisals

You deserve a medal for. . . .

I've always admired the way you. . . .

It's critical that we agree upon objectives.

What do you think of your performance?

Are you generally satisfied or dissatisfied with your productivity?

What do you think of the job in terms of variety, challenge, and security?

Do you feel you get along with your co-workers?

Where do you hope to go in this job?

What are your career objectives?

In what way can I be more helpful to you?

Receiving Performance Appraisals

I would like your advice. I'd appreciate it if you could give me a few moments of your time to let me know how you think I'm doing.

I'd like a chance to talk with you about how you think I'm doing and what my potential is.

Am I working up to your expectations?

How can I do better?

Are we in agreement about my priorities?

Is there anything you would like me to do that I have not been doing?

How can I improve on that?

Am I communicating with you satisfactorily?

Here is a list of my accomplishments.

Here are the things that have happened.

Here is how these activities relate to the objectives we set forth.

Here's what's going on now.

Here's the direction I would like to go in the upcoming year.

This is what I'm going to produce, and this is how I plan to do it. It may not always appear that I am the one who is personally going to achieve this, but these are the specifics of how I'm going to execute it.

Here are the things that didn't occur that we decided to do last year.

We didn't do 10 percent of what we wanted to see happen, so let's try to work on that 10 percent and add other objectives.

Do you agree that it would be helpful if we discuss this again three months from now?

Requesting Responsibility and Raises

Since I handled . . ., how about letting me try something that would build on that experience?

I see this problem, and I have some ideas on how we might solve it. Can I work on it?

Here's something I've uncovered in my work, and I have a proposal on how I could do something about it.

Here is an area that, it seems to me, could really help us out if we could explore it and do something with it. Do you agree?

I was talking to . . . and he said . . . Can you tell me more about it, because it seems to tie in with. . . . I think it would be worth doing.

I'm making this request for a raise because of the . . . achievement that we wouldn't have had without my work.

Since you say a raise is not possible at this time, I'm willing to work at my present salary now if we have the understanding that in three months we'll have a review of my continued accomplishments and progress.

When shall we set a definite date to check back on a salary renegotiation?

Speaking Up on the Telephone

Do you have a moment to talk?

Do you have time to speak to me now?

Is this a good time to call you?

Do you have a minute for me to give you some information?

I'm calling because you're an expert in our field—so it would be valuable to have your input.

I'm not calling to upset you, but I do want to let you know that we have some problems to deal with. I'm outlining them in a letter that I'll mail today.

After you read the letter and digest the information, you can call me back.

Thanks for the information.

Please call me back if you have any questions.

Thank-you for calling.

What can I do for you?

I have some ideas on that. Can I get back to you?

I'll get back to you if I have questions.

You just caught me. I'm on my way to a meeting and have to be there in five minutes.

My other phone is ringing. I'll get right back to you.

I have someone on the other line. May I call you back?

There's someone in my office right now. I'll cut the meeting short and get back to you.

I'm on another call. Can you hold?

Will you wait, or shall I call you back?

Can I ask you to hold a second while I see what we can do?

Sorry I had to put you on hold.

Do you mind waiting while I check that for you?

I'm still checking on that for you.

Thank-you so much for waiting.

I'll be happy to have someone call you with this information.

You caught me short, and since I'm in the middle of other business, I'd rather not give this short shrift.

I'm unable to talk to you now. But I know this situation is important to you. Will you be available at 10:00 A.M. Wednesday? I'd like to talk to you then.

I want to give this my full attention, so I'll check into it and get back to you.

I don't have that information now, but I'll be happy to locate it and call you back tomorrow.

I'll be glad to take care of that for you. Can we schedule another call on this for Friday?

I'll call you next Monday with my answer.

I'll research an in-depth answer for you and call you back to. . . .

I can see this is an important issue, and I'm not sure exactly how I want to respond on this. Instead of giving you a quick answer, which in a sense demeans the importance of what you're saying, I'd rather take whatever time it needs and call you back after giving it serious consideration.

Delivering Criticism

I'm having some negative feelings about some things you're doing. May I give you some feedback about it and tell you how I feel?

I think it's important for me to tell you about some issues that are getting in the way of our working relationship.

I'm not blaming you for my feeling. I'm simply describing how I feel.

I'm not criticizing you as a person. But a certain behavior disturbs me, and I'm saying this to help our relationship, keep you out of trouble, and improve your performance.

Taking Criticism

That never occurred to me, but I'll give it some thought.

I really don't think that's the way I react, but I'd like to consider it and then get back to you.

222

I'm glad you're saying what's on your mind. Actually, I haven't considered my views or behavior in that light. Let me think about it.

I'm willing to give what you say some thought to see what we can do about it.

Give me some time to think over what you said, so we can see how to approach it.

Acknowledging Errors or Mistakes

I'm sorry—I was wrong and I don't have an excuse.

I accept responsibility and have no excuse.

I can offer you an explanation if you want to hear it, but I still feel bad that I'm wrong.

I don't have an excuse. If you want an explanation I can give you one, but it's still not good enough—and I'm still wrong.

You have a right to feel the way you do.

Can I make it up to you in any way?

All I can say is I would never knowingly do anything to embarrass you, and I'll do all I can to make sure it never happens again.

Yes, that happened, and it was a mistake.

It was not an appropriate thing to do, and I see now if I didn't see it before that it could have been done differently.

Here's what I learned from it and what I'll do differently if a similar situation occurs.

Maybe it wasn't so bad that it happened, because I learned from this.

Here's what good will now come out of this.

Bearing Bad News

As your manager I have to warn you that you're not performing up to our standards. I'm putting you on probation. You have the opportunity to overcome the problems you're having.

It's my place to bring out the best in you, because if we can't move forward we can't proceed together.

Two months ago we agreed to meet at this time, so let's review the results of your effort and go from beginning to end to see where you stand. Why don't you start first by giving me your impression?

As you know, we've been reviewing your work and, as I've discussed with you before, everything has been written down and thought through. Unfortunately, this is the end of our working relationship.

Your last day will be Friday . . . and you'll be paid until. . . .

You will be working with . . . in outplacement, and you have an appointment with him on. . . .

You have an appointment with . . . in personnel at. . . .

We need to talk now about how you'd like to announce this.

What do you want me to tell your secretary?

Let's prepare a statement so that when you need to use the company as a reference, you'll have it.

Do you understand what I'm saying?

I can understand how you feel. You have worked hard for this company, and it's difficult to go through this situation.

I've called the staff together for some rather distressing news.

This office is closing at the end of the year.

We are taking the company in another direction, so we're planning on downsizing.

We have consummated a takeover and will now be merging with. . . .

The company is being sold.

We're restructuring the department.

Economic conditions demand that. . . .

We feel bad about this, but this is the reality.

This is not something we wanted to have happen. We'd much prefer to have it go the other way.

I'm sorry! I didn't expect this, and I'll do whatever I possibly can to help you land on your feet.

We're all in this together. I feel very bad.

Hearing Bad News

What is the specific reason for the termination?

What date will I be leaving?

How long will I be paid?

What will be the relationship between my severance pay and the contribution I have made?

What are my termination benefits?

How long can I keep the company car?

How long will my benefits be continued?

Can I purchase the company car?

Will I be given outplacement service?

Will I be provided with office space while seeking new employment and, if so, for how long?

What will the company say when I need to give it as a reference?

Will you put that statement in writing?

Answering Unwelcome Questions

Let me think about that for a moment.

If you're worried about my ability to do my job because of my pressures at home, I'd like to have a conversation with you.

I still haven't made up my mind about that—let me work on it just a bit longer.

That's really not part of this business.

I believe that's a personal matter and not relevant here.

I'm sorry—that's a personal question.

I prefer not to say—that's my personal business.

I stopped giving my age at 35.

Today I feel like a babe in arms.

Today I feel a hundred years old.

Dealing With Gossip, Rumors, and Underhanded Maneuvers

Of course, you didn't do it, but listen to what has been happening.

I'm not accusing anyone. But if gossip, rumors, and lies get out to our supervisor we'll all be vulnerable.

Let's see whether or not there's truth to it.

I don't think that was in order. My perception of you has certainly been colored by this. This may be an isolated incident, but you can bet that in the future I'm going to conduct myself and my dealings with you quite differently.

I understand that you have been saying . . .

Do you really mean what I hear you've been saying?

Why don't we talk about what you meant?

If it isn't true it won't be said anymore, will it?

I've heard that, but it's just a rumor.

I know it's not true.

Finally, there are the phrases each of us learned at our mother's knee—"Thank-you," "Please," and "You're welcome." They're so simple we often forget them in the busyness of corporate life. But when you remember to make them part of your verbal IQ they'll enhance your verbal image throughout your management career.

227

Notes

Chapter 1

1. Copeland Griggs Productions, *Valuing Diversity* (San Francisco: Film/Video Series, October 1987).

Chapter 2

1. "Slip and Gloom Index Rates the Candidates," *New York Times,* 1 November 1988.
2. Ibid.
3. Ibid.
4. Arthur W. Sager, *Speak Your Way to Success* (New York: McGraw-Hill, 1968), p. 28.
5. Sandy Linver, *Speak Easy—How to Talk Your Way to the Top* (New York: Summit Books, 1978), p. 95.
6. Ibid., p. 59.
7. Sager, *Speak Your Way,* p. 145.

Chapter 4

1. Mortimer Adler, "Are You Listening?" *American Express Cardmembers Newsletter,* June 1983.
2. Ron Stepneski, "Memos to Managers," *The Record,* 21 August 1988.
3. Donald Christman, "Effective Listening" in *Handbook of Engineering Management,* ed. John E. Ullmann, Herbert F. Holtje, and Donald Christman (New York: John Wiley, 1986).
4. Ibid.

5. Adler, "Are You Listening?"
6. Ibid.

Chapter 5

1. Henry C. Rogers, *Rogers' Rules for Businesswomen* (New York: St. Martin's, 1988).
2. Don Bagin, "Here Are Practical Ways to Help You Get Ahead," *communication briefings* 7, no. 8 (June 1988).
3. Rogers, *Rules for Businesswomen.*
4. Bagin, "Practical Ways."

Chapter 6

1. Don Bagin, "Here Are Practical Ways to Help You Get Ahead," *communication briefings* 7, no. 8 (June 1988).

Chapter 7

1. "News From Toastmasters International," Toastmasters International, Santa Ana, Calif.
2. "Loose Change," *The Record,* 9 January 1989.
3. "Polishing Speaking Skills," educational feature, International Training In Communication, Anaheim, Calif., Cat. No. 571.
4. "Speeches by Management," A Toastmasters International Program, Toastmasters International, Santa Ana, Calif.
5. *Briefings' Best Tips: Tactics and techniques to help you and your employees work smarter and succeed, Communication Publications and Resources,* 1988.
6. "Polishing Speaking Skills."
7. Sandy Linver, *Speak Easy* (New York: Summit Books, 1978).
8. *Briefings' Best Tips.*
9. Linda D. Swink, "Friendly Persuasion," *Toastmaster* 54, no. 11 (November 1988).
10. Ibid.

11. "Speeches by Management."

12. Karen Berg, "Handling the Question and Answer Session," *Toastmaster* 54, no. 11 (November 1988).

Chapter 8

1. Betty Lehan Harragan, *Games Mother Never Taught You* (New York: Rawson Associates, 1977).

2. Donald L. Kirkpatrick, *No-Nonsense Communication* (Elm Grove, Wisc.: K & M Publishers, 1985).

3. *Briefings' Best Tips: Tactics and techniques to help you and your employees work smarter and succeed, Communication Publications and Resources,* 1988.

4. Al Kelly, *How to Make Your Life Easier at Work* (New York: McGraw-Hill, 1988).

5. Harragan, *Games Mother Never Taught You.*

6. Kirkpatrick, *No-Nonsense Communication.*

7. Kelly, *Make Your Life Easier.*

8. Kirkpatrick, *No-Nonsense Communication.*

9. Ibid.

10. Kelly, *Make Your Life Easier.*

Chapter 9

1. "Loose Change," *The Record,* 9 January 1989.

2. Donald L. Kirkpatrick, *No-Nonsense Communication* (Elm Grove, Wisc.: K & M Publishers, 1985).

3. *Briefings' Best Tips: Tactics and techniques to help you and your employees work smarter and succeed, Communication Publications and Resources,* 1988.

Chapter 10

1. Philip B. Crosby, *Let's Talk Quality* (New York: McGraw-Hill, 1989).

2. Ibid.

3. Natasha Josefowitz, *Paths to Power* (Reading, Mass.: Addison-Wesley, 1980).

4. Ibid.

5. Ibid.

6. Ibid.

7. Ibid.

8. *Briefings' Best Tips: Tactics and techniques to help you and your employees work smarter and succeed, Communication Publications and Resources,* 1988.

9. *Briefings' Best Tips.*

Chapter 11

1. Henry C. Rogers, *Rogers' Rules for Businesswomen* (New York: St. Martin's, 1988).

2. Ibid.

3. Sherry Chastain, *Winning the Salary Game* (New York: John Wiley, 1980).

4. Ibid.

Chapter 12

1. Daniel Goleman, "Why Job Criticism Fails: Psychology's New Findings," *New York Times,* 26 July 1988.

2. Ibid.

3. Ibid.

4. Ibid.

5. Ibid.

6. Ibid.

7. Ibid.

Chapter 13

1. Daniel Goleman, "Why Job Criticism Fails: Psychology's New Findings," *New York Times,* 26 July 1988.

2. Ibid.

Chapter 15

1. Philip B. Crosby, *The Art of Getting Your Own Sweet Way* (New York: McGraw-Hill, 1981).

Chapter 16

1. Henry C. Rogers, *Rogers' Rules for Businesswomen* (New York: St. Martin's, 1988).
2. Ibid.
3. "Stress on the Job," *Newsweek,* 25 April 1988.

Chapter 18

1. Marilyn Moats Kennedy, *Office Politics* (Chicago: Follett, 1980).
2. Ibid.

Chapter 19

1. Henry C. Rogers, *Rogers' Rules for Businesswomen* (New York: St. Martin's, 1988).
2. Ibid.
3. Ibid.

For Further Reading

Bartos, Otomar, J. *Process and Outcome of Negotiations*. New York: Columbia University Press, 1974.

Bedrosian, Margaret. *Speak Like a Pro: In Business and Public Speaking*. New York: John Wiley & Sons, 1987.

Berry, C. *Your Voice and How to Use it Successfully*. England: Harrap, Ltd., 1986.

Chastain, Sherry. *Winning the Salary Game*. New York: John Wiley & Sons, 1980.

Corey, G. *I Never Knew I Had a Chance*. Monterey, Calif.: Brooks/Cole, 1978.

Crosby, Philip B. *Let's Talk Quality*. New York: McGraw-Hill, 1989.

——. *The Art of Getting Your Own Sweet Way*. New York: McGraw-Hill, 1981.

Doyle, Michael, and David Strauss. *How to Make Meetings Work*. Chicago: Playboy Press, 1976.

Fiedler, F. E. *A Theory of Leadership Effectiveness*. New York: McGraw-Hill, 1967.

Flesch, Rudolf. *Say What You Mean*. New York: Harper, 1972.

Gard, Grant C. *The Art of Confident Public Speaking*. Englewood Cliffs, N.J.: Prentice-Hall, 1986.

Geeting, Baxter and Corrine. *How to Listen Assertively*. New York: Monarch, 1978.

Greenburger, Francis, with Thomas Kiernam. *How to Ask for More and Get It*. Chicago: Contemporary Books, 1978.

Harragan, Betty Lehan. *Games Mother Never Taught You*. New York: Rawson Associates, 1977.

Hersey, P., and K. H. Blanchard. *Management of Organizational Behavior*. Englewood Cliffs, N.J.: Prentice-Hall, 1972.

Ilich, John. *The Art and Skill of Successful Negotiations*. Englewood Cliffs, N.J.: Prentice-Hall, 1973.

Irish, Richard K. *Go Hire Yourself an Employer*. New York: Anchor Press/Doubleday, 1989.

James, M., and D. Jongeward. *Born to Win*. Reading, Mass.: Addison-Wesley, 1973.

Josefowitz, Natasha. *Paths To Power*. Reading, Mass.: Addison-Wesley, 1980.

——. *You're the Boss*. New York: Warner Books, 1985.

Kanter, Rosabeth Moss. *Men and Women of the Corporation*. New York: Basic Books, 1976.

Kanter, Rosabeth Moss, and Barry A. Stein, eds. *Life in Organizations*. New York: Basic Books, 1976.

Kennedy, Marilyn Moats. *Office Politics*. Chicago: Follett, 1980.

Kirkpatrick, Donald L. *No-Nonsense Communication*. Elm Grove, Wisc.: K & M Publishers, 1985.

——. *How to Plan and Conduct Productive Business Meetings*. New York: AMACOM, 1986.

Kelly, Al. *How to Make Your Life Easier at Work*. New York: McGraw-Hill, 1988.

Lang, Doe. *The Secret of Charisma: What It Is and How to Get It*. New York: New Choices Press, 1980.

Linver, Sandy. *Speak Easy—How to Talk Your Way to the Top*. New York: Summit Books, 1978.

Lipnack, Jessica, and Jeffrey Stampls. *Networking: The First Report and Directory*. New York: Doubleday, 1982.

Loden, Marilyn. *Feminine Leadership*. New York: Times Books, 1985.

Montgomery, Robert L. *Listening Made Easy*. New York: AMACOM, 1981.

Rogers, Henry C. *Rogers' Rules for Businesswomen*. New York: St. Martin's Press, 1988.

——. *Rogers' Rules for Success*. New York: St. Martin's Press, 1984.

Sager, Arthur W. *Speak Your Way to Success*. New York: McGraw-Hill, 1968.

Sarnoff, Dorothy. *Speech Can Change Your Life*. New York: Dell Publishing Co., 1971.

Steil, Lyman K. *Effective Listening: The Key to Your Success*. St. Paul, Minn.: Telestar, 1982.

——. *Listening . . . It Can Change Your Life*. New York: McGraw-Hill, 1985.

Souerwine, Andrew H. *Career Strategies*. New York: AMACOM, 1978.

Tarrant, John J. *How to Negotiate a Raise*. New York: Van Nostrand Reinhold, 1978.

Index

AG4V